BRASS BAND DIGEST

Brass Band DIGEST

BARRIE PERRINS

EGON PUBLISHERS LTD
Meeting House Lane, Church Street
Baldock, Herts SG7 5BP

First Published in 1984
by Egon Publishers Ltd.
Meeting House Lane, Church Street, Baldock, Herts.

Copyright © Egon Publishers Ltd.
and Barrie Perrins

ISBN 0 905858 28 X

Printed in England by
Streetsprinters
Meeting House Lane, Church Street
Baldock, Herts SG7 5BP

Contents

General

Instructive

Technical

People

Music

Miscellaneous

Foreword

Until recent years the Brass Band Movement had inspired but few literary excursions. The weekly or monthly news sheets have given valuable service, but books dealing with our activities, though valuable, had been rare.

The movement's inward-looking exclusiveness was perhaps the reason for this. Now, however, the appeal of our form of music-making tends to be seriously accepted in 'high places', and some modern bandsmen also have a wider vision than formerly.

For these, this book will surely be much appreciated. The skilled musicianship of Barrie Perrins is well-known, and here, with clarity and economy of language, he ranges through subjects technical, historical, biographical, even philosophical with skill and understanding.

Here are writings to enjoy, and to provoke discussion — the outcome of deep research and wide experience.

Eric Ball

Introduction

For over thirty years Barrie Perrins has contributed instructive and technical articles to the brass band press. In fact, more than 600 of his articles and music reviews have now been published.

This book grew from the many requests he received for copies of these articles, although quite a lot of new material is published here for the first time.

The publishers are grateful to 'The British Bandsman' and 'The Musician' for their co-operation in allowing certain articles to be reprinted.

In this book, the author is providing a digest of aspects of the Brass Band movement, with supplementary items included to broaden its musical content. He is also attempting to stimulate progress in administrative, musical and presentation terms.

Finally, he tries to encourage general appreciation of this worthwhile form of music-making which deserves support, not only for its cultural and educational benefits, but for its contribution to the quality of life — and its enjoyment.

The Brass Band – An Introduction

(... a singularly beautiful musical medium: Eric Blom)

The Brass Band Movement began in the first half of the 19th century, with great impetus from the Industrial Revolution. Coal miners, cotton mill employees and factory workers of all kinds joined together to make bands that were springing up, a new form of musical self-expression. British choral traditions were strong, but singing did not appeal in the same way as instrumental music which already had made its mark in some degree via the Waits and itinerant street musicians. Sponsorship by factory owners (some of whom appreciated the cultural benefits bands could give, also the means to unite workers) brought funds for instruments, thus bands quickly formed throughout industrial areas — and beyond. Since then brass bands have developed much, organisationally and musically, bringing fulfilment to many thousands. From school ensembles to the highly trained bands which play in the world's great concert halls — and even featured in the prestigious series of London's Promenade Concerts!

Whether representing a village, town or principal city — or a sponsor, brass band involvement in contemporary society is considerable, at home and abroad. Among sponsoring bodies household names such as British Leyland, Fairey Engineering and Hammond's Sauce are but three, plus the many bands sponsored by The Salvation Army throughout the world.

Contests (or competitions) have done much to develop and standardise this art form, particularly concerning *instrumentation*. One band normally comprises 1 Eb soprano cornet; 9 Bb cornets; 1 Bb flugel horn; 3 Eb horns; 2 Bb baritones; 2 Bb tenor trombones and 1 Bb/F bass trombone; 2 Bb euphoniums; 2 Eb basses and 2 Bb basses (tubas) — plus percussion. This is standard British instrumentation which often varies in bands overseas. A homogeneous group of instruments (apart from percussion), they consist of two

9

families: the 'trumpet family' are bright toned, e.g. cornets and trombones; and the 'horn family' are mellow toned, e.g. horns, baritones, euphoniums and basses. Skilful scoring and use of these two families gives impressive tone colour results and effects, answering critics who say the brass band lacks tone colour! And there is precision and tonal warmth/excitement which, with other qualities, create the unique brass band sound. Design and comparable improvements have advanced tone quality and technical possibilities immeasurably, and bands of average rating only can play a large and varied repertoire, satisfying to most audiences. 'Pop', jazz, marches, light music of all kinds and classical numbers — the brass band can effectively present a wider repertoire than virtually any other musical ensemble. Original band compositions are now much more numerous than hitherto, some receiving acclaim by outstanding music authorities. The musical skill of brass bandsmen has been recognised by compositions written specifically for them by well known composers, e.g. Elgar, Holst, Ireland, Rubbra, Howells, Vaughan Williams and Malcolm Arnold. There is also a trend of more orchestral musicians (some of whom were 'cradled' in brass bands) participating as conductors, composers and arrangers. Clearly the brass band is a means of introducing large numbers of people to good music, and an on-going cultural unit.

Initial musical expression and progress is much quicker via the brass band than most other forms of music-making, and interchangeability of players adds to its usefulness, especially in the educational sphere. A thriving National Schools Brass Band Association indicates just that, moreover school bands help develop personal character, team spirit and confidence — and parallel qualities. Eric Ball, doyen of brass band composers, described the school brass band as 'a gateway to worthwhile musical experience', eminently justified by the progress of countless school band members. Community spirit can progress too through brass bands, via identification with village, town and factory, for example. In some areas the brass band is a tradition, even a 'way of life', involving two and even more members of individual families in the same band! Personal dedication in many bands is comparable with that of Olympic Games athletes — and rivalry is keen too . . . Bands provide much colour at local and national events with their rousing music and uniforms, also public service, e.g. concerts in hospitals, old people's homes and the like are regularly featured in band engagements;

10

churches, parks and schools are included too, bringing the inspiring sound of brass to almost all of our society. Town carnivals, processions and numerous civic functions would be incomplete without brass bands! Aptly called 'The People's Orchestra', the brass band is also a fellowship in itself; nor are there any class barriers: membership includes miners, local government officers, civil servants, policemen, artisans of all kinds, company executives, lawyers, housewives and even doctors. Although male membership predominates, female membership is growing steadily.

Internationally the Brass Band Movement is progressing rapidly, and bands are playing a consequential part in spreading understanding and friendship. Many reciprocal band tours take place each year; countries as far apart as the USA and Japan feature in these exchanges, in addition to numerous exchanges between Britain and European countries. Brass bandsmen are veritably musical ambassadors, and besides cultural relationships there have been trading benefits, not least in musical instrument sales!

There is an increasing awareness of brass band usefulness at a time when creative art forms are being overwhelmed by non-creative activities, and rising costs do not help. . . . A full set of instruments today costs in the region of £24,200 added to which are teaching fees, expenses for rehearsal facilities and general administrative/ maintenance costs! In many cases bands are self-supporting, but overall they have an uphill task to keep going. The basic amateur status of brass bands is a pointer to their character and spirit, formidable factors, deserving support.

The Pleasure of Playing

(Music will serve those who strive to live its harmonies: Yehudi Menuhin)

Dr. Suzuki, the well known Japanese music professor, says that through the study of a musical instrument we are able to develop more fully as human beings, and can apply the skills learned to other spheres of human activity. And it is widely recognised that release of feelings through music brings a measure of fulfilment. More specifically, brass musical instrument performance helps co-ordination of various faculties (mind, tongue, breath and fingers) which in turn promotes health; and there is increasing awareness of that among educationists and music therapists. Individually and collectively, musical activity adds much to the quality of life itself!

Playing in a brass band is a useful and creative hobby—it brings pleasure to us as we try to progress musically, and hopefully if gives pleasure to our listeners too! Besides being a gateway to worthwhile musical experience, for young and older people alike, the brass band is recognised as a musical combination of real artistic and cultural importance. No less an authority than the late Sir Malcolm Sargent, famous orchestra and choir conductor, said the brass band is one of the finest sounds in music—moreover he proved his practical interest with a splendid arrangement for band of a Mozart opus.

Discipline, team spirit, development of self-expression and personal confidence are among the benefits of playing in a band. Socially too, band membership has many advantages for we find friendship and happiness in making music together, plus an awareness of unity and achievement which is satisfying in a world whose sense of values is often confusing. And the growing brass band *repertoire* is the envy of musicians elsewhere because of its wide appeal, variety and quality.

The character of a musical ensemble is the character of those who operate within it, adding immeasurably to its effectiveness and spirit

12

when properly channelled, whether band, choir or orchestra. For example, of Dennis Brain (one of the world's greatest brass instrumentalists) Sir Neville Cardus said 'By playing proportionately in orchestras he made his genius felt'. That is *true musicianship:* to play (or sing) proportionately, with due regard for correct musical relationships. There are few who can approach the high standards of Dennis Brain; but we can ensure that our activities constitute a good influence in our bands, musically and personally.

Buyer Beware!

(When purchasing brass instruments)

The well known caveat 'Buyer Beware!' is relevant when purchasing brass musical instruments, whether written guarantees are given or not. In a *general* sense, some guarantees are not worth the paper they are written on, even if the small print is readable! It is therefore prudent to check carefully — or have checked by a competent person — any instrument intended to be purchased. Reputed dealers often permit a 'trial period' before purchase is finalized and, if during that period the buyer is not satisfied, a change may be arranged or the defects remedied without additional payment. Not all vendors are so accommodating, however.

Particular care is necessary regarding second-hand instruments — and age is not necessarily a criterion. For example, a badly maintained instrument deteriorates quickly, similarly an instrument bought from a professional musician is likely to have had much more wear than one previously played by an amateur. I once tested a euphonium awaiting repairs for one of H.M. Guards Bands and, although only 10 years old, its condition suggested it was many times that age. And an instrument made by a reputed manufacturer will normally last longer than a little known producer.

One primary consideration when purchasing brass instruments relates to *pitch*. Even though nearly all brass bands have changed to Standard Pitch (A.440 v.p.s.), a few instruments are still available in High Pitch (A.452.5 v.p.s.) of which some are not easily adaptable to current requirements.

With valved instruments, arpeggios played throughout the compass and slow chromatic passages (using all valves individually and in different combinations) will usually reveal tuning deficiencies — and leaks! External surfaces, particularly in the area of joints, require scrutiny. Slides and valves (the whole slide — inner and outer — and plugs in the case of a trombone) merit close examination too.

14

When ill-fitting or badly worn parts are apparent, an estimate for repair may be agreed and an appropriate price reduction requested from the vendor.

An instrument case is necessary for every instrument so, if one is not included, check the size required; if it is not standard, a case may prove quite expensive. Although mouthpieces can usually be adapted to fit most instruments, bore differences can occasionally make that difficult — or impossible. Mouthpiece fitment can thus prove an important aspect of purchase.

Normally a *dated receipt quoting the number of the instrument* will be given when a sale by a reputed dealer is completed. It is strongly recommended that, whatever the source of supply, such a receipt shall be obtained and preserved. Stolen instruments are often circulating and, if any doubt arises as to the *bona fides* of a vendor or any other points are in question, it may be worth the trouble to check the position with the police and/or the manufacturer of the instrument.

Comparisons and Reflections

A distinguished composer once indicated that the professional writer needs to think of the commercial value of his work rather than its quality at a time when gimmicks, different sounds and the like are, apparently, the main requirements! The disappointment and feelings generally of musicians of integrity can, perhaps, be appreciated when it is realised that our 'musically sick society' encourages quasi-illiterate, immature note-pedlars to command enormous incomes, yet genuine musicians who have had years of arduous training are out of work.

Today it is often trivial matter that receives popular acclaim, but substantial material tends to be ignored or rejected. Music copy that is printed in hundreds of thousands is frequently trash that would be disregarded by discerning purchasers, and a small minority become rich because of majority demand for it; the gramophone record industry suffers likewise!

To balance these rather pessimistic views, it is worth noting that the 'voices' of Mozart, Beethoven, Brahms and comparable composers are still heard above the cacophony of twanging guitars, yells of 'vocalists' and similar noises which daily assail us via radio and television.

Enlightenment
Although it may sound a little smug, it is possible to find enlightenment through the brass band which enables *qualitative* music and *creative* musical activity to be enjoyed. Statistics show that we bandsmen comprise only a small movement, not without problems; even so, we have much for which to be thankful and our efforts, regardless of limitations, constitute a measure of honest endeavour and musical sanity.

No less an authority than Sir Malcolm Sargent said 'The brass band is, for me, one of the finest sounds in music'; and Sir Malcolm,

Sir Adrian Boult, Vilem Tausky, Elgar Howarth and conductors of like status have actively identified themselves with brass bands, facts which speak for themselves. Our Movement's contribution to the nation's musical life is not inconsiderable, and there can be few villages or towns in Britain where the brass band is not represented; moreover there is a remarkable growth potential through the increasing interest of education authorities who recognise the brass band's value as a medium for musical instruction and appreciation.

Looking inwards — and outwards

With regard to our limitations, it is right that we should be self-critical, looking *inwards* for means to progress. To be objective we ought also to look *outwards* for ideas and be less insular in our relations with other forms of musical expression.

Brass bands have much to offer *in combination with other groups*, e.g. choirs, orchestras and small instrumental and vocal ensembles (soloists too) with whom attractive concerts may be given, thus supplementing all-brass programmes which are delightful to bandsmen but frequently indigestible and uninteresting to Mr. Everyman! Audiences are likely to be larger, and advertising and other costs shared, if this idea is applied; and there are added economic advantages in providing concerts jointly with church and school choirs, as church and school premises may be utilised.

We can do a lot to improve our administration, presentation, public relations, economic position and associated matters: in other words MAKE THE MOST OF WHAT WE HAVE!

The First British Brass Band

Details are often requested about the first brass band to be established in Britain, and the following information may help to prove the name of that elusive ensemble!

For a considerable time it was assumed that New Mills Old Prize Band, said to have originated in 1812, was the oldest brass band in Britain. The Coxlodge Institute Band of Durham was founded in 1808, however, and it subsequently operated as the Coxlodge and Hazelrigg Colliery Band which later became the Wallsend Rising Sun Colliery Band.

An intriguing event took place in 1821 when, in order to celebrate the sinking of a shaft at Gosforth Colliery, a ball attended by nearly 300 people was held 1,100 feet underground at the shaft bottom, and the Coxlodge Institute Band provided music!

On 10 June 1962 a correspondent wrote in *The Observer* that the Nottingham City Guild Brass Band could claim to be at least 200 years old. He added that the town chronicles show that in 1759 it played an 'antheme fore the joyous tidings' of Wolfe's victory at Quebec!

It seems unlikely that any one of those bands was an all-brass ensemble at its inception for, according to The *Brass Band Movement* (J. F. Russell and J. H. Elliott published Dent), the first brass bands were formed in 1832. Several brass bands date from the early 19th Century but they originated as reed or mixed wind instrument groups.

In Dr. Sydney Northcote's book *Making Your Own Music* (Phoenix) reference is made to the formation of an all-brass band in Blaina in 1830, and another in York a year later. And Dr. Harold C. Hind wrote in a book titled *Waits — Wind Band — Horn* (Hinrichsen): 'It is not possible to state with real accuracy the exact date of the first amateur band consisting entirely of brass instruments. Blaina, Monmouthshire, is said to have started such a band in 1832, but other records say 1823; Daniel Hardman, one of the Waits of York, formed a brass band in 1833. . .' Another authority, Kenneth Cook states in his book *The Bandsman's Everything Within* (Hinrichsen) that 'An all-brass band of 20 players was in existence at Brown's Ironworks, Blaina, in 1823'.

Although dates conflict, from the foregoing and band history recorded elsewhere, it would seem a reasonable assumption to regard the Blaina ensemble as the first brass band established in Britain — that is, until precise information proving otherwise is available!

Let's have a Brass Band Museum

Suggestions for a Brass Band Museum have been made during the past decade—so far without any positive results!

That a museum has not already been established indicates lack of vision in numerous quarters, especially when regard is given to the Movement's colourful history extending to well over a century, and the abundance of material for such a project. Besides stimulating interest in brass bands and providing necessary research facilities, a museum would have incalculable public relations' benefits.

A museum specifically for the Brass Band could accommodate manuscripts, records and tapes, instruments, personal property of outstanding conductors, composers, bands and soloists, books and general information, all of which would be educational and worthwhile in a general sense. If the premises were large enough, brass instrument demonstrations, lectures, recitals and even band concerts could be included in its scope.

Obviously sponsorship by a responsible body would be required at national level, not only to establish but to *maintain* it. And it could conceivably become self-supporting, even commercially viable, thus companies interested in brass band affairs who give support might reasonably expect some return.

In this context attention is drawn to the existence of redundant church premises which are sometimes available at little more than site value, furthermore a church could be adapted to serve museum purposes with minimal alteration! There is also the possibility that property at present held on trust deeds *but not fulfilling the purpose of their provisions* might, subject to Charity Commission or other relevant approval, be used for a National Brass Band Museum. Alternatively, if a property wholly available for museum purposes is *too* ambitious at the present time, perhaps a *room* in an existing central building (in London or Manchester, for example) could be offered as a beginning by an interested party?

Clearly the establishment of a museum worthy of our Movement is becoming increasingly desirable and, once agreed in principle by a duly recognized body with practical ideas and people prepared to work on the project, it is likely that the necessary material would be quickly forthcoming.

Band Associations, Music Publishers, Musical Instrument Manufacturers and Dealers, with others, are invited to consider the subject with a view to positive action being taken—and soon!

Towards Wider Musical Horizons
(Not all the music is in the notes . . . Mahler)

Brass band members are sometimes criticised for being musically insular because they seem to have little interest in other forms of music-making! Certainly many of us have a tendency to be so immersed in our own sphere that we fail even to observe other musical activities, thus a measure of criticism is justifiable. Admittedly time-limitation means we cannot always exercise the interest we would wish, but that is not necessarily a valid reason . . .

At a recent lecture, the well known trombone virtuoso Don Lusher recommended listening to all types of music, and he said we should not be narrow-minded in that context! From such a highly respected musician, that is advice worthy of consideration; and we can widen musical horizons via *listening habits* particularly.

Reading too can enlarge knowledge, for 'Reading is to the mind what exercise is to the body'. The varied selection of musical literature (including scores) available in public libraries is not always appreciated; furthermore, skilled library staff are normally willing to assist in book and music choice. And if material is not immediately to hand, the required item may be obtained in due course at minimal cost. Reciprocal nation-wide arrangements between libraries make virtually every book and music opus in stock available to all, regardless of locality.

Band public relations are enhanced by exercising interest in other forms of music-making e.g. in choirs, orchestras, operatic societies and the like, with mutual advantages including personnel interchange. At a time when the general recession is hitting cultural activities hard, there may be financial benefits too. Liaison with churches and schools can likewise be beneficial, in regard to advertising and hire of halls.

22

Publicity

Publicity for band events often leaves much to be desired, yet local press and civic authority news controllers are usually prepared to assist, at little or no cost. Additionally, education authorities may be prepared to include band concert details, for example, in lists of educational functions. And support generally can be achieved by *imaginative* advertising.

The repertoire we present to listeners is another area wherein we can widen musical horizons — ours and theirs! The quality (and variety) of our programmes frequently leaves room for criticism, and the content of some programmes indicates that little thought has been given to music selection. Many bands have substantial music libraries, yet only the proverbial 'tip' is utilized. There may well be hidden, as yet unplayed, treasures in band music cupboards which, besides freshening concerts, could revitalize motivation! Methodical purchase of *new* music at regular intervals is also recommended: to develop musical outlook and to encourage composers, arrangers and publishers; hopefully increased sales will *improve printing standards* in certain quarters too! Participation of guest ensembles and soloists — singers and instrumentalists — to feature as added attractions in band concerts, will give a broader musical spectrum to our efforts and extend listener-appeal.

Hymn Tunes

More methodical and *purposeful* band rehearsals, with clearly defined aims such as tuning, tone and technique improvement, could usefully be employed instead of the 'play-through' approach adopted in more than a few band rooms ... Hymn tune playing for a few minutes at each rehearsal, an idea used by numerous eminent ensembles for tone and expression development, is specifically recommended.

It is a welcome fact (and significant) that better qualified musicians, conductors and players, are coming into our Movement to whom we must give support. There is also a growing number of band members showing interest in composing and arranging who deserve encouragement similarly: to play their works, and to occasionally conduct us. The 'John Smith' of today may well become an 'Eric Ball' of tomorrow! And the few minutes of rehearsal time allocated now to an embryo composer/arranger may later yield musical harvests — *and widen musical horizons.*

Could Do Better!

Igor Stravinsky (1882-1971) was regarded by many as the greatest composer of our time. His viewpoint that:

> 'In music, more than in any other branch of art, understanding is given only to those who make an active effort; passive receptivity is not enough'

is therefore worth pondering.

The same applies in rehearsal as well as performance. For example, a certain conductor is renowned for (among other questions) asking at poor rehearsals whether or not his musicians have brought their minds with them!

Just as it is possible to look without 'seeing', it is possible to produce notes without 'playing the music', i.e. the required effort is not being made. Nobody can maintain 100% concentration all the time, but there is a need for self-discipline and 'participation' before understanding (and therefore progress) can be achieved.

Several ensembles come to mind who exemplify this 'participation' quality, who give listeners (and themselves) a satisfying, uplifting feeling which makes their programmes extra-ordinary. Performances that are *remembered* invariably embody that quality, when control, musicianship and artistry combine into one great unity of purpose. Such a degree of 'participation' is the result of much hard work in preparation and dedication — and the ensuing balance and blend make the music really live!

Running a Band

Probably the greatest contributory factor to our happiness in brass bands is found in the way they are run, i.e., their administrative arrangements. There are bands that are *musically* first class but they do not *enjoy* activities as much as less musically efficient bands, and enquiry often shows that this is due to administrative differences. Admittedly band administration presents problems but it can be made less difficult if certain objects are observed, not the least being simplicity; and a practical Constitution is the first essential.

The aims and functions of the National Brass Band Club are probably known to most bandsmen, and any problems referred to the Club regarding administration are competently dealt with by the Secretary. The N.B.B.C. will provide a specimen Band Constitution, adaptable to local requirements, on request; this document has been thoughtfully prepared with a view to practical application and it meets our needs admirably.

Among other things, administration covers personal relationships, a most important consideration in any collective unit of endeavour, and it is in the interests of each bandsman to ensure that the band to which he belongs is properly administered. It is not unknown for bands to be run by two or three individuals (instead of Band Committees) which, in addition to being undemocratic, may lead to undesirable results even more detrimental to welfare and progress generally. Any authority given to individuals in a properly administered band is delegated by the Band Committee who, of course, have power to withdraw such authority if the need arises.

Whenever reading of the dissolution of a band or about the loss of members, the question arises: 'Was this due to faulty administration?' Of course, each member has a part to play in observing standards of conduct and co-operation, but *efficient administration* will promote this. Rules and discipline are necessary if we are to get the maximum out of our music-making, and the happiest bands are those that are properly administered, even if they are not 'rated' musically! The happiness of a band is more important, for example, than contest success; happiness is indeed a criterion, in the musical sphere and elsewhere. Financial control is another important aspect and it is occasionally the cause of dissension when administration is questionable. Not a few Public Subscription bands have proved that the brass band can be a self-supporting, thriving concern, but effort is, of course, necessary!

Age should not be regarded as a yard-stick in considering the appointment of Band Officials, and young members ought to be encouraged to participate in band management. In addition to the usual Officials, it may be beneficial to appoint a Public Relations Officer. Clearly the person appointed as Secretary has to be a very capable person, e.g. imaginative and tactful and able to apply his authority fair-mindedly, for Band Secretaries (like Contest Adjudicators!) bear unenviable powers and responsibilities which demand these, and other, qualities. Morale and musical enthusiasm will quickly diminish if concert/contest arrangements are inadequate, another pointer to the need for efficient administration.

The Band Committee is an integral part of our Movement, and discerning Committee members will accept their duties thoughtfully; moreover, the confidential nature of subjects sometimes discussed in Committee imparts considerable responsibility and trust. Regular meetings, at least once a month, are advisable, for they help to 'keep the pulse' of feelings in a band, and encourage members to bring appropriate matters before the Committee. It is desirable that all business, other than that which is purely routine, shall be approved by the Committee, and in the case of major issues by the band as a whole. Concise summaries (in Minute or other form) of Committee meetings should be recorded for future reference and guidance. Some bands depend on external support, particularly in respect of finance, and suitable persons and local organisations can, therefore be co-opted on the Committee; band representation can usefully be effected on local organisations' committees similarly. It is important that co-option shall be carried out carefully with particular regard to fair representation and voting powers. Beware political intrigue!

A 'Ladies' Committee', subordinate to the Band Committee, may prove valuable and bring the family spirit into band affairs. Wives and girl friends (even daughters and sisters) may thus give assistance in a tangible, official way although not actually participating in administration. Socially a Ladies' Committee is an asset and it enables our women-folk to share our activities. There are instances when this idea has been applied which have proved feminine ingenuity and enterprise to be most helpful in raising funds and in organisation generally!

Recording band history is an oft-neglected item. As well as recording annual membership statistics, details of concerts, contests, fêtes, carnivals, processions, etc., and other events in which bands feature may be recorded. Band photographs taken at regular intervals will promote personal interest and can be effectively reproduced on programmes. Some bands publish brochures which include historic details, an idea worthy of consideration too.

Making Ourselves Presentable

Band Presentation is frequently criticised, not always unjustifiably, and it is hoped that these points will help improve matters.

Visually the brass band is not particularly attractive to 'Mr. Everyman' and we must, therefore, make the most of what we have! The following suggestions are not complete, i.e. there are probably many others, but they are fundamental to the subject and their application may increase the enjoyment of our audiences.

1. The positioning of chairs for a concert can advantageously be made the responsibility of two band members whose task ought to be completed before anybody else is allowed on stage. Compact seating aids blend of sound, it also ensures that the players give the appearance of belonging to the same band and that they look 'tidy'. The movement on stage of a band, whether arriving or departing, can best be effected as a *team* and each player ought to know his approximate position beforehand so that quick assembly and dispersal are achieved with the minimum of disturbance. When a soloist is featured he should have his entry, playing position and exit route clearly in mind before performing.

2. Guard against delay of any kind as there is nothing so destructive to the interest of an audience. If each item is ready as soon as its predecessor had ended, a 'flow' of activity is realised and programme continuity maintained.

3. Behaviour on stage should be carefully controlled; full concentration is neccesary from each band member for the maximum effect. (Unnecessary conversation and movement are absent from events that are well presented). The demeanour of a band has considerable visual and psychological value and it is eminently appropriate to develop a *happy* spirit in our activities instead of the 'Wish we hadn't come' feeling apparent sometimes. . . .

4. The question of an interval during a concert is a controversial issue, and it may be advisable to leave its consideration to conductor

28

(or compère) who should be able to 'feel' the needs of the audience, as well as the band, at the time. The interval in a programme can cause loss of interest and even listeners; on the other hand one may be necessary for the bandsmen. When an interval is decided upon it should be announced and the time allocated scrupulously kept.

5. The usefulness of percussionists in band (and orchestral) programmes is becoming increasingly evident, and they can contribute a great deal to presentation. Assuming they are competent players, much can be said for their being in a *seeable* position during performance. Continental bands, particularly those in Switzerland, feature percussionists as soloists; and the inclusion of drum 'breaks', for example, provides attraction and variety for audiences. This is a matter in which composers and arrangers can help as well as imaginative conductors.

6. The 'dress' question is one for commonsense application but, if there are offenders, the capable Bandmaster will have sufficient authority (and tact) to remedy the situation. Clean instruments literally add brightness; moreover, instruments that are clean respond better than those that are not! It is a good rule for a band to be in playing position a few minutes before a programme commences when the bandmaster can personally check the visual effect.

7. The practice of bandsmen standing as the conductor arrives on stage is something which, if done well, impresses an audience and gives a measure of dignity (besides showing respect) in concerts.

8. A printed programme has much presentation value and may even be the deciding factor of *attendance* for some people. Simplicity, clarity and attractiveness in design are paramount considerations, and any suitable items (e.g. publicity for other cultural events) known to be of local interest can be included.

Presentation is complementary to Programme Compèring and Programme Building; if all three are done efficiently there will be little cause for criticism.

Compèring Concerts

(Bright is the ring of words when the right man rings them: Robert Louis Stevenson)

The way in which concerts are compèred has considerable bearing on listeners' impressions, quite apart from musical results, and forms an important part of band presentation. The compère is a 'bridge' between band and audience and he is, in effect, a Public Relations Officer. He obviously needs to be informed, observant and articulate if he is to help the atmosphere of an event and stimulate listeners' interest.

Frequently band concerts are compèred by conductors, many of whom make a good job of this additional function, but regrettably there are exceptions — even for some of the best known bands. Efficient conductors are not necessarily efficient compères (the reverse also applies), and the position should be remedied in such cases for it can quickly spoil reputations.

Many conductors find their musical responsibilites quite sufficient and would prefer to be relieved of the onus of compèring concerts, but tradition tends to force continuance of both functions. A suitable alternative could probably be found among band members — and might conceivably lead to the discovery of hidden talent! There may well be a third cornet player, for example, with the required gifts of expression and personality; and he would no doubt welcome this opportunity of specialisation and service.

The delightful compèring of Robin Boyle, in *Friday Night is Music Night* and numerous other radio and television programmes, is a splendid example. His quick wit and thought-provoking comments invariably add much to listeners' knowledge and enjoyment of concerts at which he officiates.

Is is better for a compère to over-estimate rather than under-estimate the intelligence of an audience, therefore repetition and inconsequential 'patter' should be avoided. Imagination, intelligent anticipation and sense of humour are essentials for a compère, for application of those qualities helps to make concerts 'live' — and also helps cover gaps and delays which occasionally arise. . . . Unless details are included in printed programmes, it creates interest if some history of the relevant composers and their music is briefly mentioned, and the discerning compère will acquaint himself of such facts (if not provided by band administrators).

When a soloist participates, it is better to quote his Christian and family names rather than refer to a solo by 'T. Brown'; and any interesting or unusual (creditable!) characteristics a soloist may have can also be detailed. A little humour often adds to the appeal of a concert, and a good compère will be able to assess listeners' requirements.

Whenever titles of music are in a foreign language it is most desirable that the compère shall know correct pronunciation if it is proposed to announce them in that form. Likewise, if a *translation* is to be given, it should be accurate. Unhappy recollections abound of one famous conductor's oft-given announcement of the overture to 'Die Zauberflöte'; fortunately his band's performance invariably relieved the mystification so caused! Yet another conductor is amusingly recalled for his countless assertions that the *translation* of 'Berceuse de Jocelyn' is 'Angels Guard Thee' . . .

The demeanour of a compère is important: he should not only try to radiate cheerfulness, but should give the impression he is glad his band is appearing; music is above all to be enjoyed! What a compère says affects, in no small measure, the *mood* of players and listeners, e.g. he can do much to relieve tension and remedy problems which frequently arise at concerts, particularly on 'big' occasions.

If brass band concerts are to attract and *hold* the interest of the general public, the rôle of compère is one aspect that must never be neglected!

Thoughts on Brass Band Leadership

The proof of a good conductor is in making something of indifferent material but there is a quality in conductorship that goes even further, that inspires and brings forth 'great and unforgettable performances'.

The late Major George Willcocks of the Irish Guards and Black Dyke Mills Bands typified this quality in both the brass and military band spheres, and he will long be remembered not only for 'the Dyke's' beautiful interpretation of the overture to *Le Roi d'Ys* (Lalo) but countless other performances to which it was applied. Major Willcocks had remarkable tact and sense of communication with musicians which helped bring out the best in them, and he infused a vitality into music which made it sparkle.

Few of those present at the Royal Albert Hall Brass Band Festival Concerts in October, 1962 will forget Eric Ball's leadership of Liszt's *Les Preludes*, and evidently George Thompson (with Grimethorpe Colliery Band) led a similarly inspired performance of Wagner's *Rienzi* at the 1963 North Eastern Area Contest. However, many other renderings of the same works by comparable bands fail to impress — and the difference clearly rests on *leadership* whose inspiration endures, as indicated.

Adequate definition of leadership is difficult but it has contributory factors, not the least being *conviction*. Competent conductors have to know what they want (as well as the way to get it!) and the best ones generally possess strong personalities and assured ideas which inevitably 'connect' with performers and listeners; personality projection, with due regard for composers' wishes, is one of the main facets underlying 'interpretation that compels' and is largely responsible for music's variety. Respect, which should ideally be shared by 'leader and led' in any group activity, is also a valuable attribute of this quasi-magic quality.

There are probably fewer out-standing leaders in our Movement today than there were, for example, in pre-war years but the position has to be related to prevailing circumstances. Higher musical standards and the social-economic revolution of recent years have increased the *demands* of leadership which, regrettably, fewer people are prepared or sufficiently dedicated to accept; current conceptions of discipline also have bearing on the subject. . . .

An uncontradictable fact about *worth-while music-making is the conductor's unity with his musicians.* If every bandsman earnestly sought this ideal, leadership would be easier and there would be more likelihood of 'great and unforgettable performances'!

Contesting

Since the beginning of time Man has engaged in competitive activity which has, in countless ways, proved stimulating and contributed to progress. Healthy competition in any sphere can be a good influence by giving 'edge' to performance and allowing fair comparisons to be made; it also appeals to sporting instincts. Competitive activity must be well controlled, however, otherwise subversion may destroy its purpose and principles.

In the musical field the competitive element can be beneficial, and brass band contests (although tending to fill up the calendar with events not always meaningful) often encourage and further the legitimate aims of participants. Even so, there are advantages and disadvantages in contesting, and we can usefully question our motives when considering the subject.

Contesting is a means to an end — not the end itself; it provides incentive for greater effort and ideally makes available independent, constructive criticisms of performance, besides valuable experience in meeting and hearing fellow musicians. Repertoire, technique and musicianship generally can be enhanced in this way, and morale may be boosted too when success is achieved! The growth of the Brass Band Movement owes much to contesting, not least because of the introduction of new music and raised standards of musicianship, and the Movement would be poorer without it.

Regrettably contesting can become a vehicle for personal pride, a trophy-hunting expedition accompanied by the 'anything-they-can-do-we-can-do-better' outlook which sometimes develops into an all-consuming sickness, eroding both musicianship and enjoyable music-making . . . Although friendly rivalry is frequently met, in not a few cases fierce rivalry without regard for friendliness, 'one-up-man-ship', tensions and obsessions ensue — with relative happiness diminution for those taking part. That sad situation becomes a 'rat-race', and contests then become a be-all-and-end-all of band activity, with prestige and self-glorification the prime objectives. From personal experience and observations it is clear that contesting has occasionally been the cause of bands breaking up and friendships ending, in addition to other comparable adversities; the subject should not therefore be viewed lightly.

To help remedy the disadvantages of contesting, some guidance can be obtained by deciding initially what proportion of time shall be given to contests as distinct from other band engagements. Balance in this respect may well provide the key to greater effectiveness. An honest assessment of time spent on contest work may reveal a preoccupation therewith which, in spite of some benefits, can be detrimental to bandsmen's interests and progress generally. Careful selection and pre-planning for contests will also help avoid problems.

These comments apply to contests for soloists and small ensembles as well as band events. Undoubtedly our attitudes to contesting largely determine the advantages — or disadvantages — in participation: and that is a thought well worth pondering!

Conductors of the Future

It has been said that every soldier has a Field Marshal's baton in his knapsack. Due consideration may suggest that a parallel metaphor is equally true: that every bandsman has a conductor's baton inside his instrument case! Just as soldiers have ideas about becoming Field Marshals, undoubtedly bandsmen have ambitions to be conductors, which constitutes a logical sequence of thought.

There is an increasing awareness of the serious shortage of qualified conductors, and it is made more acute by the rising demands (musically and otherwise) on conductors today. We can therefore usefully ask ourselves: Are we doing enough to encourage and train those within our Movement to undertake conducting responsibilities?

It is common knowledge that, in not a few cases, band leadership is monopolised by one or two people who jealously guard their control, keeping out any rivals for the baton. . . . On the other hand it is fair comment to mention that the onerous duties of conductor are often shouldered by 'faithfuls' who, although recognising personal deficiencies, continue in that capacity because nobody else is able (or willing) to accept those duties. Whatever applies, however, the ideals, purpose and *effectiveness* of a band are closely linked with its leader.

One of the saddest situations in this context occurs when young players, whose enthusiasm and knowledge are of inestimable value, are prevented from obtaining conducting experience because of prejudice within their bands, e.g. from older people who refuse to allow what they feel is 'power' to be exercised by other than members of their own age group! This 'power complex' (it arises in numerous comparable activities) is perhaps understandable — but *unreasonable;* it also stifles progress and leads to all kinds of problems. Age is not necessarily a criterion of ability, and worth noting is the growing number of young people in bands who pursue music studies methodically and take qualifications, also the existence of progressive bands and Associations who provide facilities to help and train potential conductors, regardless of age considerations.

Embryo Barbirollis and Boults may well be within our ranks and we must not fail to (a) recognise their usefulness and influence, and (b) encourage them, if the brass band movement is to progress as it could — and should!

Audience Appreciation

Hans Keller, one of Britain's most eminent music critics, once wrote:
'The difference between a crowd at a football match and a concert is that most of the football fans know the rules of the game.''
That is worth pondering in relation to band concert (and contest) audiences.

Executive musicians are frequently deceived by listener-response, even when they know within themselves that their efforts have not merited such reaction — which can operate either way! For example, when tempo is increased at the end of certain items a warm audience response is engendered, yet when that same material is played more musically and without (unmarked) tempo change, reaction is less noticeable. Similarly, many soloists know the kind of solo (and additive) that sends some listeners into ecstacy and, although at the time revelling in applause received, such soloists may admit afterward that it was not a really *satisfying* experience. This proves, with few exceptions, that anything gained cheaply usually relates to the price paid. . .

The *Allegro* movement seems to encourage more observed listener-response than the *Adagio*, even though the latter is probably more demanding in overall control and performance terms, and its musical effectiveness likely to last longer. Balanced programmes can usefully contain both kinds of material, however.

Referring back to Mr. Keller's statement, any tendency to underestimate the knowledge of listeners must be avoided! But how can the desired result be achieved? Initially, the answer is in sincere self-analysis, then consideration of informed comment from external sources. The whole spectrum of music appreciation and assessment is, admittedly, subject to fashion and other extraneous factors, but there must always be overriding considerations of appropriate repertoire and *quality* with musicianship and skilled presentation, if anything near the optimum is to be realized.

Musicians worthy of the name have various responsibilities: to communicate; to entertain; to enlighten; to convince; to inspire and to educate. There are others, but for brevity reasons only these are mentioned. In band programmes there is room for all kinds of music, moreover standard brass band repertoire offers a remarkably wide area of choice.

Do we give sufficient consideration to rehearsal techniques, performance standards and the repertoire we present? And could our motives be improved? These matters affecting listener-response are worth considering!

Private Rehearsal

(Prepare well, and then enjoy it! — Don Lusher)

A conscientious bandsman will recognize his duty to practise privately whenever possible, and he will appreciate that the ensuing benefits will be felt not only by him, but by the band as a whole.

Private rehearsal should be methodical and regular and — at least until a good standard has been attained — under the supervision of a teacher, preferably an exponent of the instrument proposed to be studied. (Take care in your choice of a teacher, and remember that 'letters after a name' and soloistic prowess do not always indicate teaching ability!)

The frequency and duration of private rehearsal are matters of personal adaptation, but it is better to have short rehearsals often rather than occasional rehearsals of long duration. Lengthening rehearsal time gradually is a good way to build endurance, but the accent ought not to be on 'time spent rehearsing' but on 'what and how one rehearses'. Never rehearse beyond the stage of tired lips!

Record

It will be found useful to plan rehearsal time in advance and to keep a record (pencilled dates on exercises are recommended) in order to check progress. Although many book tutors claim to be complete, experience shows that few are — and they often overlap and supplement each other. Careful selection is therefore necessary to prevent waste of time and money; beware of publications that promise 'fantastic results' within a few weeks, even if they bear pictures of famous soloists!

Progressions in book tutors should not necessarily follow the order in which they are printed; it is preferable for exercises to be adapted to the needs of the student, hence the desirability of a teacher. Methods of instruction vary, and the fact that one tutor suggests a different approach from that advocated by another does

40

not indicate that either is wrong. Physically it is possible to travel to a given point by different routes, and this also applies musically. It is desirable for melody pieces to be introduced to the beginner as circumstances allow, so that interest will not flag; fatigue must never be allowed to outweigh interest!

In many ways we are creatures of habit and it is therefore important to ensure that we acquire good habits. Posture, breathing, fingering, etc., are matters which eventually become 'natural' to brass instrumentalists, but there is a danger in taking them so much for granted that we fall into bad habits unconsciously. It is easier to learn a good habit than to unlearn a bad one, and this demands attention in private rehearsal.

Tone production must never be neglected, regardless of one's ability, and exercises for tone cultivation and control are recommended in all rehearsals; they are useful for 'warm-up' at the commencement of each period. Indeed, many reputed artists invariably begin in this way. Definite attack and release help tone clarity; slow melodies played *pianissimo* throughout, then with 'hairpins' (*crescendi* and *diminuendi*); and long, held notes played in varying dynamics are excellent tonal exercises

The fundamental requirements for private rehearsal are found in practising exercises on the following: tone cultivation and control; scales; mixed intervals, slurred and tongued; arpeggios throughout the whole range, slurred and tongued; all varieties of tonguing.

Some players devise a 'warm-up' exercise which includes each of these technique facets — a commendable practice provided it is not done mechanically. Technique is the servant of music and not the end in itself; it is therefore possible to be good technically but poor musically. Always play exercises thoughtfully — never mechanically — for there is often musical shape and interest in them even if at first they seem to be just notes.

Intonation is of major importance to all musicians, particularly to brass players who have a wide 'margin of error' possible in addition to the temperature hazard which affects tuning. (Intonation relates to the player, tuning to the instrument.) Arpeggio and scalic exercises can help intonation as well as develop articulation and agility.

Volume control is just as important in exercises as in other music and, even when dynamics are not indicated, it will make efforts more interesting and *musical* if dynamic contrasts are made. Generally exercises should be played without *vibrato*. Avoid playing too long in one register to the detriment of the others. Air support is necessary at all times with control via the diaphragm; and phrase appropriately.

It is worth devoting some time to sight-reading at, say, every other rehearsal, and try to keep variety in key signatures so that unusual keys will not present problems in public performance. For an average player the following could be used as a plan for a forty-five-minute practice period:

10 minutes: exercises on tone cultivation and control.
10 minutes: scales with varied articulations.
10 minutes: *arpeggios* and mixed intervals, slurred and tongued.
5 minutes: chromatic exercises in duple and triple rhythms.
10 minutes: sight-reading.

When you are practising what appears to be difficult music and the desired results are not obtained within a reasonable time, it is better to leave that particular work until a subsequent rehearsal rather than apply the 'keep-at-it-'til-it's-right' idea. Awkward sections can frequently be overcome when approached with a fresh mind (and lip) and there is little to be gained in spending what may be a disproportionate amount of time on a few bars — a view that will probably be appreciated by one's family and neighbours! Complicated passages become much easier to play if they are first broken down in their rhythmic groups and practised separately; rhythm is indispensable to a musician, for without it music loses shape and becomes meaningless.

Limits

Especially where soloists are concerned, it is advisable for private rehearsal to include music of greater difficulty than that proposed to be played in public, thus providing a measure of technique 'in hand' and greater confidence than would otherwise be available. It is a failing of some soloists to attempt material which is either beyond them or makes such demands that they are stretched to the limits of their ability during public performance.

Whenever possible, rehearsal with a competent pianist is recommended, for this is a useful discipline and it helps develop musicianship; solo repertoire can be built in this way too.

Style development is a major consideration but, in addition to learning about this elusive quality from players of repute, it is better to develop a *personal* style than merely to copy others. Try to project your personality into playing, but not so that the intentions of the composer are disregarded, of course! Knowledge of the words (where applicable) and the history associated with a piece of music helps interpretation. Remember too that personal standards may require compromise in regard to *tempi*, which can with value be checked occasionally with a metronome.

Particularly when playing slow melodies, strive after the 'song-style' and avoid the jerky, sectionalized approach adopted by not a few soloists and due, in many instances, to a mistaken conception of phrasing and clarity requirements. Each solo ought to be viewed as a whole and performance of it *in its entirety* as often as possible is recommended accordingly. Try to think of your instrument as being part of you, rather than just a machine on which music can be produced!

Purpose

Purposeful rehearsal demands all the faculties and it should never be attempted when physically or mentally tired. Eric Ball, writing on systematic study, recommends, 'Be mercilessly self-critical and don't be afraid to ask for advice,' and this applies to beginners as well as to established musicians. It is said that we move either forward or backward musically but, although this view is often proved, there is sometimes an interim STATIC period when we consolidate what we already have.

Economic use of rehearsal time should apply always and the intelligent student will ensure that each minute is fully utilized. Variety is essential to interest, so avoid too much repetition; exchange of material with other players is recommended in addition to experiment with works from local libraries which often contain treasures. Don't limit your choice of music to that written for your own particular instrument; be adventurous! As well as rehearsing alone it will be found enjoyable and musically rewarding sometimes to join others in duets, trios and similar small ensemble music-making.

Rehearsal should be enjoyable; and if prepared well, *results* should be even more enjoyable!

Band Rehearsal

Ideas vary concerning effective band rehearsal, and it is fitting to periodically consider this aspect of our activities with a view to improvement. The quality of performance depends largely on the quality of rehearsal — yet rehearsal technique is often neglected, resulting in loss of motivation and interest generally.

Band rehearsal usually takes place once or twice a week, and clearly *preparation* is necessary if we are to get anything like optimum results from our efforts. Not least is the need for *mental preparation:* we should be in the right mind for rehearsal, to be receptive and willing to co-operate with our conductor and fellow bandsmen, and so give of our best as members of the 'team' in a spirit of mutual respect.

One celebrated conductor occasionally puts the question 'Have you brought your minds to rehearsal?' — which apparently has the required effect when minds are wandering! Preparation for band rehearsal includes private practice, to ensure that each player is 'acquainted' with his instrument and therefore able to cope with band requirements.

Time of arrival is important. If rehearsal is due to commence at 8pm it is well worth arriving a few minutes earlier, if possible, to assist with preliminaries such as chair positioning, music and music-stand placement.

Some conductors begin each rehearsal with scales and a few hymn tunes; this constitutes a valuable 'warm-up' and tuning check, and also enables late arrivals to join in quickly! Whatever the commencement arrangements, rehearsals need to be planned. The advice in a pre-war monthly journal, *The Bandmaster,* is worth quoting in this context: 'It is a bandmaster's duty to stir up not only enthusiasm but *imagination* in the minds of his men.' A standard rehearsal lasts 2 hours, a useful period in which much can be accomplished if conditions are good; on the other hand, inattention and interruptions can quickly reduce actual playing time and rehearsal benefits . . .

Attention during rehearsal is vital. Effective rehearsal demands all our faculties, and ideally we should be in a reasonably fresh state to concentrate and therefore respond appropriately. Sometimes musical enthusiasm overcomes discretion, and we discuss problems among ourselves instead of addressing questions to 'the man in the middle'; self-discipline is essential for progress in any group activity, and it also enriches personal relationships.

Without a sense of humour life can be very dull, and to be able to laugh at ourselves is part of our tradition, wherever we are; but we must be careful not to cause offence or to ridicule each other during rehearsal.

Selection of music for rehearsal has considerable effect psychologically and on rehearsal enjoyment generally. A varied repertoire is normally preferable to just one work during a whole rehearsal, regardless of how qualitative one particular work may be; and fatigue must never outweigh interest — a cogent factor where wind instrument performance is concerned. Experienced conductors usually know just how far rehearsal on a specific opus can continue. However, in the case of less experienced leaders, discreet indications can be given by Band Committee members whose authority has relevance in this context.

To frequently stop a band to check mistakes is one sure way to wear down patience and lose response; and 'sterile perfectionism' should be avoided. It is more economical to stop once and draw attention to several points than to keep stopping for each individual point — furthermore a 'look' at an erring player will probably suffice to indicate his mistake instead of stopping the full band to explain!

Each rehearsal should ideally include some new material, if only for sight reading development; it is also a way to extend repertoire.

Whether or not a 'break' period is observed is a matter for local decision; if one is agreed, it should be strictly adhered to so that time used is minimal. The question of smoking during 'break' is also a matter for local decision. In addition to increasing fire risk, smoking tends to prolong any free period granted, and it may also cause discomfort to non-smoking band members.

It is prudent to allow a few moments for band announcements about engagements and other matters; written confirmation can also

45

be given via a Notice Board in rehearsal premises or by detail slips handed to members.

The band librarian may require assistance at rehearsal for distributing and collecting music which, if methodically done, can save an appreciable amount of time. Care in handling music is very important (especially when music cost is considered) and any damage observed should be reported immediately to the librarian so that repair or replacement can be quickly arranged.

When a resident conductor is not available it may be appropriate to invite a guest conductor in his place rather than cancel rehearsal, i.e. if a deputy is not available within the band. Among other benefits, this will increase a band's flexibility provided the substitute is competent, and it may stimulate appreciation of the resident conductor's work too.

Break-down of difficult passages of music can usually be done in full rehearsal. If, however, that is not practicable, a 'section rehearsal' may prove helpful. Split the band for (say) 15 minutes: conductor to deal with the difficult passages in an adjoining room, and his deputy to deal temporarily with the remainder of the band. If only one room is available, a particular section rehearsal may prove necessary at a different time. This section rehearsal idea is successfully operated by many bands, thus enabling specialized instruction; basics such as articulation, enharmonic fingering and tone production can also be attended to at a more personal level.

Regular checks of band tuning, posture and presentation, for example, assist in keeping a band up to standard. Seating formation too can be experimented with at rehearsal so that *visual* as well as aural results are assessed. Analysis is an ever-present requirement in effective rehearsal!

Good conductor-playing relationships contribute to good rehearsals, and qualities such as tact, tolerance, understanding, positivism and bandsmandship all have a part in personal and musical communication. Should friction arise between members, it is desirable that any disturbance shall be minimal, hence the relevance of good discipline and strong band administration. Committee members have a responsibility in this area where mature outlook and diplomacy are required to resolve matters satisfactorily. Choice of a good march to end rehearsal when problems or disputes have arisen will probably prove therapeutic and show that, even if we cannot achieve absolute unity *personally*, we can unite *musically*!

When rehearsal has ended, prompt action in clearing away music, chairs and other items of equipment is a task with which conscientious members will assist; it 'seals' the evening's activity and leaves things clear for another period of enjoyable, purposeful music-making.

Reflection and observations suggest that the rôle of conductors in the wider sphere of *musical education* is sometimes lacking. More than a few conductors regard their duties only in terms of leadership, i.e. relating to the music played, but others accept responsibilities in the broader sense of musical education. It is hoped that reference to these two approaches will stimulate discussion thereon and, perhaps, lead to higher standards of musicianship; how to widen our musical horizons (not forgetting purposeful reading) is something we can profitably think about.

These are but a few thoughts of which consideration could yield appreciably better results from band rehearsal. Let us remember too that our attitude to rehearsal will largely determine the benefits from it!

Ingredients for Good Brass Playing

John Fletcher, tubist of the London Symphony Orchestra and the Philip Jones Brass Ensemble listed the following ingredients that go into making a good brass player:

1. Decent equipment
2. Physical wherewithal
3. Desire and determination
4. Intelligent, hard work
5. Good instruction
6. Regular exposure to higher standards
7. Regular opportunities for performing

They are points that teachers and players can usefully ponder! Moreover, they apply to most, if not all, wind instrumentalists.

Too often in the past, inadequate equipment has been supplied to music students, and even today the view that 'anything does to learn on' is occasionally heard. Although top grade instruments are not absolutely necessary until high standards of performance have been reached, instruments should be of good quality otherwise results may be prejudiced.

Playing brass musical instruments makes varying demands in physical terms. Such activity can be of considerable benefit in developing physique and general co-ordination, an important factor in the music therapy sphere. With regard to general music performance, particularly rehearsals and programmes of long duration, care should be taken to ensure that players have adequate physique to support the demands made. This applies especially when young people are involved.

Clearly, desire and determination are necessary for progress in any serious activity. And *intelligent* hard work will similarly enhance results.

With few exceptions, good instruction is vital if musical progress is to be achieved, whatever the medium. *It is easier to learn good habits than to unlearn bad ones.* Frequently bad habits are allowed to continue and worsen because they are not checked by competent instructors. Posture, respiration, intonation, tone quality and phrasing are but a few aspects of brass instrument technique which indicate whether or not tuition has been good — allowing for lazy and indifferent students, of course!

Regular exposure to higher standards, as performers and listeners, constitutes an important factor in musical education. To play constantly with others of the same or a lower standard can lead to disinterest and boredom which in turn erodes musicianship, whereas playing with other musicians of higher standards will stimulate interest and progress. And much can be learned about all aspects of musicianship if high standards of performance (vocal and instrumental) are intelligently listened to and assessed via recordings, radio and television programmes and live concerts.

Regular opportunities for performing are valuable for musical development, giving 'aim' toward particular events, providing incentive and personal confidence, and by raising general interest levels. *Regular rehearsal* complements this point. And the old idea of 'a little and often' is much better than irregular rehearsals of long duration. Remember too that *fatigue can outweigh interest,* hence the need for thoughtful preparation and varied rehearsal repertoire.

Some Hazards of Playing Brass Instruments

Players of brass musical instruments have peculiar hazards and problems. It is therefore prudent to consider them sometimes and share conclusions—possibly with mutual benefit.

The mental attitude towards musical problems, as with other kinds, largely determines the results in trying to overcome them. Moreover, mental and physical inter-relationships have special importance for brass players because of the very personal nature of performance involving the co-ordination of mind, breath, fingers and tongue.

One particular hazard is *mouth dryness/dehydration,* a condition many players experience. This may be remedied by:

(a) use of a throat spray;
(b) drinking water, if time permits! (Only recently I observed a well-known euphonium player drink, between movements of a solo, from a plastic bottle attached to his instrument — a good idea!)
(c) rocking the lower jaw and biting the tongue to induce saliva;
(d) clearance of the saliva ducts.

There is virtually nothing that can compare with *valve malfunction* for demoralizing a brass instrumentalist! Fortunately the relatively new monel valves give a smoother, more efficient action than bronze and brass-plated valves; but any valve can stick if it is not cleaned and lubricated properly, or if finger action is inaccurate.

Replacement of valve springs can improve action, yet more than a few players fail to recognize the possibility of metal fatigue in that context. Some even take pride in using springs of pre-World War Two or comparable vintage. . . . And noise from springs can often be eliminated by reversing their position.

Valve lubrication is best effected by use of water or oil; if the latter is used, apply a reputable product — and *sparingly* for optimum

50

results. Always ensure that valves and cases are properly cleaned before lubrication, with particular attention to guides and tacquets. Other than in an emergency, the unhygienic (and damaging) practice of expectorating on valves can never be justified.

A further cause of valve malfunction can be worn or ill-fitting corks and pads. If new ones are fitted, be sure they are of the correct size.

Leaks also constitute a hazard. If a leak is suspected, first examine the water-key corks where air loss frequently arises due to wear and bad fitting. The relevant slide or tubing can be filled with water, and if any escapes, the remedy is obvious. Leaks elsewhere usually require the services of an instrument repairer. If leaks are located, however, they may be patched temporarily with sticking plaster or a similar agent.

Dents, especially large ones, should receive a repairer's attention as quickly as possible because they almost invariably affect tuning and, if not dealt with expeditiously, may deteriorate with even more serious results.

Clean instruments invariably play better than dirty ones! And that applies internally as well as externally. Silver-plated instruments present few problems in this respect. Soap and warm water (with the aid of brushes for cleaning inside tubing) will usually suffice, plus the use of an impregnated cloth (prepared chalk—'whitening'—for badly stained surfaces) to give a good finish externally.

Unplated brass instruments, lacquered or not, require more care; and dealer-recommended cleaners are available and effective. A warm water bath once every few weeks usually keeps instruments clean and grit-free, and a mild disinfectant can be added occasionally.

Slides require periodic lubrication, with white Vaseline or another reputable agent. *(This, of course, does NOT apply to trombone slides.)*

Mouthpiece care is important. Few people, if any, would accept an unclean cup from which to drink; yet many brass players disregard the mouthpiece parallel to that situation! Unclean mouthpieces often result in lip soreness and worse problems. Plating should be renewed if wear is apparent. Ideally, mouthpieces should be washed after use; and cylindrical brush use ensures throat and backbore cleanliness. If the instrument case does not include mouthpiece storage, the mouthpiece is best kept in a separate protective cover when not in use.

51

Choosing a Mouthpiece

Pianists often tend to have a complex about piano action, some woodwind instrumentalists are known for their 'reed fixations', and numerous stringed instrument players are constantly searching for better strings. Similarly, many brass instrumentalists possess a 'mouthpiece mania', seeking the mouthpiece which, they think, will be a panacea for all their problems!

Certain representatives of the commercial world are not slow in exploiting this weakness; and their advertisements for mouthpieces are expressed in the most 'catching' terms for which the undiscerning purchaser falls in less time than it takes to transfer five-pound notes from one side of a counter to the other. ... The 'six-octave mouthpiece' and 'All you need for a golden tone' are parallels to selling gimmicks used by unscrupulous vendors, who add insult to injury by offering even 'better' possibilities via gold-plated products which (as if you had not already guessed) cost more.

At least one famous trumpet teacher is known for making it a condition that one of his recommended mouthpieces shall be bought before he will accept a student for lessons, another example of exploitation not by any means unique.

Mouthpiece selection is a *personal* matter and what suits one player is not necessarily appropriate for another. Subject to possible embouchure abnormalities for which individuals may require correction, any marked departure from standard patterns will have mixed results, e.g. a very deep cup may improve the quality of *low* register notes, but it will probably adversely affect sound and increase tone production difficulties in the *high* register; a very shallow cup will most likely have the opposite effect.

If the rim is too wide and flat it will give the player greater endurance but also a dull sound, less sensitivity and possibly less accurancy in the high register; conversely, a rim that is too narrow and curved will cut the lips and lessen endurance; it will also improve embouchure selectivity by increasing the player's mouthpiece grip.

There is no magic in any particular mouthpiece; rather, to quote Harold Brasch, 'Mr. Euphonium' of the U.S.A.: 'It is the man behind the gun' that counts! Informed (non-commercial) advice on choice is recommended when in doubt. Hopefully a *standard* numbering system will eventually apply to all makes of mouthpiece.

Provided other considerations are equal, there seems little (if anything) to be gained by expending money on different mouthpieces once a reasonably serviceable choice has been made; moreover, constantly changing mouthpieces is a bad habit. Inquiries of several reputable brass players show that each has used the same mouthpiece for fifteen or more years, the wisdom of which is clearly shown by experience.

Instead of experimenting with different mouthpieces, the way to greater efficiency may well be found through that old, proved formula: *HOME PRACTICE!*

Soloists: With or Without Music?

'The best soloists always play without music' has been a popular assumption for many years, yet some of the greatest musicians play in public with music copies before them. George Eskdale, Dennis Brain and Albert Sammons were among the finest exponents of trumpet, horn and violin respectively, yet they frequently played publicly from music; and Léon Goossens, acknowledged by many as the world's outstanding oboist, has played 'with copy' in televised programmes. There cannot, therefore, be anything detrimental in playing thus if these and comparable artists have done so.

Sir Adrian Boult, in his book, *Thoughts on Conducting*, wrote 'Many more concerto players are now using their music at performances, even though they hardly look at it' which suggests that the copy is not without value.

Repertoire

If soloists were always to play in public without music it would mean that their repertoire would almost certainly be limited, and it could conceivably lead to monotony for both players and listeners.

Variety is musically desirable, and mass-communication means such as radio and television have added to its importance. There are musicians like Alfredo Campoli, once called 'the man with a million notes in his head', who memorized eight concertos for public performance by the time he was seventeen years old; but these are exceptional, and the majority of soloists have neither the time nor the aptitude for such feats.

Communication

Undoubtedly *presentation* is enhanced when soloists play without music, and *communication* between performer and listeners is likely to be more quickly achieved. Conversely, the result can be spoilt because of nervous tension and mental strain when playing from memory, and what should be musical may become mechanical and distorted; moreover, even the best musicians have memory lapses!

Admittedly it is possible to put more into a performance when the mechanics of reading are dispensed with entirely; there is also psychological and visual benefit in not having any 'barrier' between the soloist and his audience. Nevertheless, other factors must also be considered, not least the performer's mood at the time and the character of the music.

Apart from *presentation* value, then, there would not seem to be any special virtue in playing solos without copy, and it is really a matter of personal taste. A soloist ought not, however, to 'follow the dots' slavishly to the exclusion of all else; provided there has been adequate rehearsal beforehand, the copy is but a reminder to the proficient soloist, and his approach can be assured (and relaxed) accordingly. When music is used, care should be taken to ensure that the copy does not exclude listeners' view of the soloist or obstruct his sound.

Coda

There is always a possibility of accidents arising, such as music being mislaid or forgotten, and I well remember an incident involving a trombonist and his accompanist; their music was left in a train but they played the programmed items—and brilliantly—from memory.

Preparedness for such eventualities is recommended.

Brass Band Sound

(. . .fill the air with the most beautiful vibrations possible: Philip Farkas)

The sound of a good brass band is probably its most attractive feature, for listeners and players alike! Listening to that sound is, for many, a thrilling experience: with immediate impact, its fresh, 'open' quality is unique — if sometimes criticized for alleged lack of tone colour. And its particularly 'personal' character derives, probably, from the close personal relationship brass players have with their instruments, necessary for co-ordinating faculties during performance. The wide disparity between top class bands and those of lower grade relates primarily to *sound quality* difference, i.e. quite apart from other considerations.

In his book *Music in England* (Pelican) Eric Blom described the brass band as 'a singularly beautiful musical medium'; and the late Sir Malcolm Sargent said it is one of the finest sounds in music. Lilla M. Fox wrote 'The band movement with its pride and colour, and the incomparable sound of brass which can play the clown, call to battle, and open the gates of Heaven, all in one piece of music' (*Instruments of Processional Music*, Lutterworth Press). These and many more brass band impressions relate directly to *sound*, thus the subject merits analysis.

Of all music-making media, brass instruments provide the widest range of dynamics: they can be played so softly that listeners may have difficulty in hearing them — and so loudly that listeners may wish they had *not* heard them! The many varied articulations, tone textures and moods possible give considerable scope for desirable 'pictures in sound', with much 'light and shade' — and sensitivity. This has parallels in all the art forms: e.g. a painting by a reputed artist may contain as many as a dozen different shades of any one colour; similarly in the world of literature there are countless shades of expression in words used by the best authors and poets, making the overall result interesting and worthwhile.

In a world bedevilled by noise, where *quality* is replaced by monotonous and tasteless *quantity*, decibels (musically expressed and otherwise) have more consequence than may be appreciated, not least on health. And beauty in sound has a part to play, sometimes with therapeutic effects. In that context there is a story about the sound of a Salvation Army band which changed the attitude of an intending suicide 'from desperation to hope' (*The Musician*, 17 March 1979 refers). Innumerable examples of music's healing power (not all as dramatic as that story) can be given, and Music Therapy as a subject is becoming increasingly recognized; furthermore, the recognition of brass band sound in that sphere is more than a little significant.

The traditional brass band sound has been enriched during the past thirty years or so by the introduction of large-bore instruments, i.e. in comparison with those used previously. Other instrumentaal developments have included tuning and design improvements which have extended technical possibilities for players. Those advances have stimulated composers and arrangers, with impressive results on band repertoire — also *sound*.

Informed comment outside the Band Movement has agreeably mentioned the change in repertoire 'bringing new sound to the medium with much wider appeal'. What was a rather 'uniform' sound (with some exceptions) has become varied! That brass bands could be placed near the top of the 'Pop Charts', e.g. Hanwell and Brighouse and Rastrick, was a noteworthy development preceded by excursions into 'pop' music by (among others) Hendon Band of London. Arrangers including Siebert, Huckridge, Morrison, Richards, Farr, Langford and Broadbent have popularized the medium immeasurably.

In the classical and original band music areas, arrangers and composers such as Ball, Denis Wright, Frank Wright, Howarth, Horovitz, Snell and Gregson have similarly contributed much toward recognition of the brass band and its distinctive sound. Particular reference must be made additionally to Elgar Howarth, one of the world's busiest orchestral conductors, and indefatigable champion of brass bands who was largely responsible for their invitation to participate in London's famous Promenade Concerts. That was an outstanding achievement, not least because of prejudice in certain areas — which rapidly changed to admiration. And one music critic wrote after the first brass band 'Prom.' appearance in 1974: 'Brass band sound has clearly "registered"!'

Playing at a high volume is usually regarded as easier than playing at a low volume, but all levels of sound have to be cultivated to enable flexibility, contrast and expression; and sound should always be of even quality. Irrespective of volume, *attack* and *release* must always be definite — two more aspects of the brass band's special effectiveness. The tubist of one of Britain's best known orchestras once described the precision of his ensemble as equal to that of a first class brass band which, he asserted, is praise indeed! Conversely, another orchestral brass soloist compared his orchestra's sound with that of Grimethorpe Colliery Band playing the same material: and clearly he preferred that band's 'vibrant, exciting sound'.

The sound of an ensemble is the *collective result* of sound produced by those comprising that ensemble. Balance and blend of sound are therefore important factors in performances of quality. When a good sound has been acquired, the way to control and project it needs careful attention if resources are to be used intelligently. The fine balance and blend of sound of the best bands is frequently due in part to imaginative placing of players (not necessarily in 'standard' formation), and experiment accordingly can prove valuable. Honest self-criticism, individually and collectively, is a constant requirement to help achieve and maintain good sound, balance and blend. Moreover, if the player next to you cannot be heard, be assured that you are playing too loud!

Fingering Technique

The fingering of valved brass instruments is, admittedly, simpler than that of woodwind, keyboard and stringed instruments, yet faults and problems of brass players can, in not a few instances, be traced to incorrect fingering. Control rests to a great extent on 'fingering technique' but it is often neglected—and not by novices only.

It will be appreciated that the clearance between valves (pistons) and their cases does not permit much dirt or other impedimenta to collect before action is prejudiced, thus cleanliness and lubrication are important. It is hoped that either clean water or a good valve oil is used for valve lubrication, *never saliva* (other than in emergency) which attacks metal and is unhygienic! On the assumption that instruments are well made and properly maintained (regrettably some are not), valve operation devolves wholly upon *players*, hence the purpose of this article.

Valves are best operated by the top pads of the fingers in as natural and comfortable a position as possible; in no circumstances should valves be controlled by any part of the fingers lower than the end joints, and the top pads of the fingers ought to be just over or resting lightly upon the centre of the respective valve tops when in playing position. If instruments are held so that valves are in as near perpendicular a position as comfortable, force of gravity will assist action; instrument-support is best provided by the left hand so that the right hand is free for fingering purposes, i.e. so far as standard 3-valved brass band instruments are concerned. To achieve required results the 'travel' of valves must correspond with the line of their cases; any bias or pressure to one side will adversely affect 'travel' and cause sluggish action, even complete stoppage. Valves are, for all normal purposes, meant to be fully open or fully closed and any intermediary position is therefore incorrect, moreover they should be manipulated definitely, evenly and quickly.

It is necessary to ensure that a sufficient quantity of breath is used: this is particularly important in semiquaver passages which can become 'lumpy' instead of even, flowing groups if breath support is lacking. *Adequate breath support* is vital to all wind instrumentalists and it is especially relevant when tone clarity and continuity are analysed, matters closely allied to fingering technique.

Careful, regular practice of chromatic passages and exercises in extreme keys, tongued and slurred, will quickly improve and equalize finger action as well as help co-ordination of mental, breathing, tonguing and fingering functions, essential for precision and smoothness. Rehearsal of so-called 'technical' solos is another way to improve fingering technique and promote fluent execution.

Try to make *finger-rhythm* match the music; to the competent player this comes automatically but initially it requires conscious effort. There are instrumentalists (including some with many years' experience) who lack a methodical approach to fingering technique, and the effect of oft-practised bad habits becomes inescapable, so the ability that conceivably could be theirs is not realized.

Occasional practice of exercises employing the following valve changes will develop finger reliability, independence and speed of operation: 1 to 2; 1/2 to 2/3; 2/3 to 1/3; 2 to 3 and 1/3 to 2. The third (or 'back') finger is usually the weakest, and exercises in the keys of A Major and E♭ Major (and relative minor keys) in particular will help to strengthen it.

Music that is at first difficult to play because of fingering problems can usefully be broken down and practised in sections; experiment with different fingerings, slowly at first, then with increased tempi until the optimum fingering is finally decided. Provided this is done intelligently with due emphasis to rhythm,, the results can be astonishing!

Knowledge of enharmonic (or alternative) fingering has considerable value for band players and soloists alike because it aids tuning and renders apparently difficult music easier to play and more *fluent*. The best tutors and study books usually include exercises with enharmonic fingering, particularly useful when playing trills and long florid passages. The article on enharmonic fingering by Ken Smith in 'Brass Today' (edited by Frank Wright, published by Besson) is recommended as one of the finest expositions on the subject.

There are more fingering problems for 'lower brass' players than, for example, cornet and horn players because euphoniums and basses have much longer valves and greater weight burdens with which to cope, also much longer air columns to control, increasing co-ordination problems. There is too the extra (4th) valve to consider which, if 'Compensated' system, enables the complete chromatic compass to be played plus improved facility, sound and tuning.

Fingering technique of valved brass instruments has little resemblance to 'press button tuning' operation of radio and TV sets! There is still need to *play in tune*, i.e. intone correctly, which does not arise with valve use only. Good intonation involves *mental* and *physical* faculties, thus the competent performer has to 'think' and 'lip' notes in tune. The most expertly tuned instrument can be *played* out of tune. . . .

Fluent, 'easy' execution is an indication of a true artist; and one of the greatest contributory factors to attain that standard is *correct fingering technique*!

Double and Triple Tonguing

The ability to double and triple tongue is the 'Everest' of many brass instrumentalists, and often it is an overrated aspect of technique. It is, however, advantageous and a necessary part of the complete soloist's equipment, and useful for players who do not aspire to soloist-status.

Briefly, it simplifies the playing of quick passages in music, and can be used to provide effects which are not possible with the ordinary method of articulation. Jean Baptiste Arban (1825-1889) claimed to have been the first cornet soloist to use this articulation system in 1848, but it was applied extensively before then by flautists. Arban realized its effectiveness and he pioneered its use in several cornet/trumpet solos, the most popular of which is his arrangement of variations on 'Carnival of Venice', still regarded as a classic. Although a generation or so ago double and triple-tonguing technique was used by a select number of soloists only, the improved technical skill of brass players today permits its effective inclusion in several works for full band.

Double and triple tonguing are effected by the use of ku/ka action in combination with the normal tu/ta action (double tonguing in duple rhythm and triple tonguing in triple rhythm), and are generally indicated with the letters 'T' and 'K'; thus double tonguing is indicated T-K, and triple tonguing indicated T-T-K- (or T-K-T-). *Clarity and tone quality* are the most important considerations when questions on articulation arise, and they should be the deciding factors when alternative methods are available.

When using this technique — as in all forms of articulation — rhythmic accent requires attention, but additionally the 'melody notes' should be emphasized when playing variations on a theme so as to achieve optimum results. Because of the remarkably fast tempi obtainable with this technique, particular care is necessary to co-ordinate tongue and fingers to maintain clarity. Numerous book tutors include exercises from which students can learn double and triple tonguing, and solos employing these articulation forms are recommended for study purposes. As different from other technique aspects, these forms ought not to be started slowly; if the action is attempted at speed, the knack will be more easily acquired! The ku/ka action may take more time for some to learn than others but, if difficulties are encountered, practice with the mouthpiece only will probably prove helpful. Some students find triple tonguing easier than double tonguing, and the order in which they are learned is, therefore, a matter of personal adaptation.

It has been said that double and triple tonguing spoil tone but my experience does not substantiate that view. Of course, if an instrumentalist neglects tone production and concentrates on what might be called 'note gymnastics', the result will be obvious. . .

Dangers of Routine

'Routine — the death of music!' was one of the shortest and most pungent comments made by Arturo Toscanini (1867-1957), the eminent conductor.

Toscanini's words echoed in my mind when, at the height of the summer concert season a few years ago, I heard a programme by one of Britain's best known military bands. During some pre-concert conversation two of the band's soloists obviously anticipated a poor performance and they excused that possibility because 'we have been playing this programme for the past five weeks'. Clearly routine had killed their interest in that particular repertoire, and those feelings were shared by their fellow-bandsmen. Perhaps needless to say, the overall result was unmusical and disappointing. . . .

Output (musical and otherwise) can reach bankruptcy limits, and repetition is known to be an extraordinarily powerful enemy of musicians. Even so, outstanding artists such as John Lill, Yehudi Menuhin and Mstislav Rostropovitch, for example, bring a freshness — 'a rebirth' — to works they have played probably hundreds of times before! That Pablo Casals could say at the age of ninety-three years, 'Each day I am reborn. Each day I must begin again', is a lesson in approach to music — and life itself; it is a renewal that defies shallowness and shows an awareness of real values. Artistic (and spiritual) vision increases immeasurably when the will to renew and create is present; it also constitutes an attitude/response which restores and improves balance — especially at times of loss.

Much music heard today is 'manufactured' rather than created. Ridden with clichés, it gives the impression of having arrived on a 'note conveyor belt', *the product of routine*. In welcome contrast there is the kind of composition which is the fruit of true craftsmanship and thought — *music of substance* — bringing joy, inspiration and enrichment to the lives of both performer and listener.

Routine can bore and even frustrate; it may also diminish thinking capacity. Perhaps the late John F. Kennedy had considered its effects when he said, 'We enjoy the comfort of opinion without the discomfort of thought' — a view with numerous contexts! And routine can cause function deprivation too, e.g. by overcoming 'purpose' with 'programme'. It is so easy to become victims of duty, allowing what we do to become meaningless and part of a 'routine'.

Routine has been called a disease, cramping life, yet in countless situations and spheres routine is unavoidable! *Therefore we must guard against its effects.*

Vibrato — Its Use and Misuse

Vibrato is one of the most controversial aspects of music performance, for singers and instrumentalists alike. By definition vibrato is a slight and more or less rapid fluctuation of pitch for expressive purposes'; and it should not be confused with tremolo which is the 'rapid reiteration of a single note or chord without regard to measured time values' (Grove).

An American music authority, M. Schoen, called vibrato 'a fundamental attribute of the artistically effective singing voice' — and universally acclaimed singers demonstrate that truth. Edward Kleinhammer, distinguished American trombone professor, refers to vibrato as 'a seasoning used to accent the flavour', an opinion endorsed by numerous reputed brass and woodwind players and teachers throughout the world. Fritz Kreisler, the eminent violinist, introduced during the early part of this century the idea of continuous vibrato on every note (see *Musical Instruments Through The Ages,* edited by Anthony Baines); and experts said that Kreisler's artistic vibrato made his remarkably appealing tone even more captivating. Conversely, the vibratoless playing of Josef Joachim, another internationally famed violinist, was described as academic and dry. Clearly correct use of vibrato contributes much to tone production by singers and instrumentalists, giving vitality and character, improving expression and overall effect.

There is therefore a strong case for using vibrato in both vocal and instrumental spheres. It is used less by wind instrumentalists than by string players, however, and there are national trends: for example, wind instrumentalists trained in France and Russia tend to use more vibrato than their counterparts elsewhere. John Wilson, former euphonium professor at the Royal Military School of Music and a renowned tubist, observed that 'Vibrato is a tool in a box of tools — and the same tool is not used for every job.' Some brass players use vibrato after reaching a note, playing it 'straight' initially; another idea is to commence notes marked *diminuendo* with vibrato and taper them off with 'straight' tone, thus providing interest, colour and contrast in performance.

Ideas about vibrato vary with individuals, also in the numerous branches of music expression. In jazz groups, instrumental vibrato is more frequently used and is much wider than that in symphony orchestras, and it is comparably disparate between jazz and 'straight' singers. In jazz and light music spheres its skilled use by e.g. John Dankworth (saxophone), Cleo Laine (vocal), Don Lusher (trombone) and Stephane Grappelli (violin) is notable.

Sidney Ellison, trumpet professor at the Royal Academy of Music, differentiates between vibrato used by brass players in symphony orchestras and those in brass bands. In the former very little is required and mostly a straight, unwavering sound is produced other than for certain solo passages. Discreet vibrato is acceptable in brass bands, to be used very sparingly. Mr. Ellison suggests that in chord work absence of vibrato improves effect; he stresses need for control and recommends hand — or finger — vibrato for cornet and trumpet players.

Defending vibrato use in brass bands, a well-known Salvation Army bandmaster (and professional trumpeter) wrote that some players straighten their tone so much that the result is a cold, metallic sound which has the effect of killing the emotional content of the music. Adding to that view, the late Dr. Denis Wright once said that during a continental tour his attempts to form a brass band from orchestral brass players were unsuccessful due primarily to unsatisfactory sound resulting from vibratoless playing. It should be appreciated that orchestras have strings producing vibrato on virtually every note of sufficient duration, whereas wind ensembles have to provide their own vibrato for colour and contrast. 'Straight' playing can cause loss of lyrical quality.

John Fletcher (London Symphony Orchestra and Philip Jones Brass Ensemble tubist) suggests vibrato use by lower brass players should be treated with caution, especially when fulfilling their supporting role as bass instruments. But in any solo capacity its use should be fully investigated within the musical context. Mr. Fletcher believes that vibrato should be *inside the tone*, natural and not superimposed, which he admirably exemplifies. The superb tone, with or without vibrato, of another lower brass player — the late Alex

Mortimer — principal euphoniumist of Foden's Band, was also a splendid example.

Excessive vibrato is sometimes heard, descending to a jelly-like wobble and offending good taste; and it can become a mannerism! Opera singers are occasionally known for this, delightfully illustrated in a Gerard Hoffnung cartoon: a tenor onstage operating voice control knobs, one labelled 'Wobble', situated in his capacious tummy region. . . . Undoubtedly vibrato is damaging if uncontrolled and excessive, especially to intonation, and if the pulse is too slow it can give insecurity impressions.

In ensemble, vibrato is generally less than when playing solo; and in some music it is not required at all — for the avoidance of doubt it may be marked *senza vibrato*. Competent musicians know that vibrato can improve effect, adding warmth and helping the flow of sound; but there is need to know when it is *not* appropriate: in much repertoire of the classical period, for example, and many of Wagner's works. Regrettably some brass players/teachers have little or no regard for this facet of technique, and therefore lose colour, contrast and expression possibilities. In his book *Trombone Technique* (OUP) Denis Wick says 'The ability to make a beautiful, controlled vibrato is a very necessary part of a trombonist's technique', a view equally applicable to other brass instruments. Mr. Wick recommends slide vibrato for trombonists, but details diaphragm, lip, throat (not recommended) and head vibrato as other methods. Personal experience indicates a further method — vibrato by slight movement of the jaws: it is used by several reputed lower brass players for whom alternative methods are deemed inapplicable or inferior. Method is a matter for personal choice and, provided the result is artistic, there should be no problem. Even so, in this as in other matters, informed advice can be sought.

It was intriguing to read in a record review of the late celebrated violinist, David Oistrakh, that he 'coloured the solo line with vibrato subtleties which achieved a speaking eloquence'. And I well remember Casals, the great cellist, refer in a master class to the importance of vibrato sublety. Paul Tortelier, eminent contemporary cellist, wrote: 'The vibrato mustn't be noticed—just something to warm the tone — to bring to the tone the spirit of the music. . . .' Clearly vibrato should be well centred, never wide and throbbing like a wow-wow-wow which is inartistic and unmusical — even if (as a bassoon professor once observed) the perpetrator can reckon on being in tune for part of the time!

Evelyn Rothwell stresses the importance of controlling vibrato in her book *Oboe Technique* (OUP). She says it is vital to practise and play sometimes without it, and to acquire real control over vibrato so that it is your servant and not your master, also to be able to use it at varying speeds. The vibrato use by James Watson and Maurice Murphy on both cornet and trumpet is a fine contemporary example of what Lionel Tertis (great violist and teacher) said: 'Above all, the vibrato must be sincere and must express the inner feelings of the player'.

To summarize: Discretion, feeling and musicianship decide when (and to what extent) vibrato shall be used; it has to be related to the music being played, and always controlled. Competent instrumentalists are able to play with — and without — vibrato. It is prudent to experiment before deciding on a particular method (although different methods may be used to meet different requirements); and study the sound texture and vibrato of reputed artists, vocal and instrumental, then seek the qualities observed. A natural, well-centred vibrato inside the tone should be aimed for so that purity of tone is maintained at all dynamic levels. Sparingly and artistically used, vibrato contributes vitality and expression qualities, adding colour, contrast and interest to performance. It is but one facet of technique, however, not appropriate to every opus.

Percussion in Brass Bands

Short definition of percussion: Collective name for instruments in which a resonating surface is struck by the player.

The view that 'If Johnny can't play a brass instrument he can always play the drum' was once widely accepted. Fortunately it is rarely (if ever) heard today due, probably, to the rising status and recognition of the importance of percussionists. Percussion in contemporary brass bands does not mean only the pitchless element such as side and bass drums, triangle and cymbals: it now includes tympani and most of the varied instruments used in orchestral percussion sections, i.e. in many bands. And it has been said that percussionists can 'make or break' a band's efforts, so the power within their grasp should not be treated lightly!

Composers and arrangers are noticeably making increasing demands on percussion, and the effectiveness achieved generally seems to justify those demands. High standards of musicianship, also mental and physical agility, are therefore required from percussionists.

In his book *Full Orchestra* the late Frank Howes mentioned a Boys Brigade drum quartet (two side drums, one tenor and one bass) he adjudicated in an 'own choice' instrumental class of a music festival. This quartet competed against a pianoforte trio and a string quartet, and Mr. Howes wrote that the percussionists were 'easily the best performers', a courageous statement having regard to the amount of prejudice, instrumentally speaking, against percussion at that time. Hopefully that incident will give encouragement (and ideas!) to fellow craftsmen. Instrumental prejudice is pointedly described in the well known story of 'Tubby the Tuba' — and there are brass band percussionists who have experienced similar feelings to Tubby for the same reason. . . .

In recent years percussion has become acceptable in band contests, happily, which is equitable and proper as percussionists enjoy full band membership and should not therefore be excluded from contest participation. Nor is there any cause for thinking that percussion might cover or spoil delicate music, i.e. if the conductor knows his job.

For many years the Salvation Army popularized percussion in its 'Drummers' Fraternal' festivals which helped clarify the position, and proved the usefulness, of percussion. Many S.A. bands have excellent percussion sections whose artistry is worth hearing and *seeing*. *Presentation* is something oft neglected in band concerts, and much presentation value can be achieved with imaginative use and positioning of percussionists. In this context Grimethorpe Colliery Band — whose percussion features are exemplary — immediately comes to mind, also the Philip Jones Brass Ensemble.

Descriptive and dramatic effects possible with intelligently applied percussion are limitless, and the great master's scoring indicates this, e.g. Mozart, Handel and Berlioz. It is significant that the famous drum beats from Beethoven's 5th Symphony were used during the Second World War years as a BBC news signal, and will be remembered by those to whom it gave hope and courage. Also worth noting is the fact that Beethoven's Violin Concerto (regarded by countless listeners and players alike as the favourite) commences with four solo drum beats. Vaughan Williams introduced interesting and unusual percussive effects which have been used and developed by his successors in the orchestral sphere. And there is a great deal of film and theatre music which admirably utilizes the unlimited qualities of percussion. Certainly the crispness, dynamic force and appeal of much band and other music would be considerably lessened without percussion!

It is hoped that these few comments will help toward percussionists and brass players being regarded as equals in the Brass Band Movement. The percussion section is no longer the Cinderella of the brass band!

Far Ranging Sound

Music extending over a wide compass is generally more colourful and interesting than that written within a limited compass — provided gimmickry and comparable influences are avoided. On the other hand, however, some of the most beautiful melodies have been contained within as small a range as one octave, for example the delightful *Cradle Song* of Johannes Brahms.

For the average brass musical instrumentalist a compass of up to two-and-a-half octaves is a reasonable expectation, but for advanced players and soloists a much wider compass is possible — and necessary. In his book *Play the music, play!* (Salvationist Publishing & Supplies Ltd.) Brindley Boon refers to an Australian named Tom ('Mudgee') Robertson who could play five-and-a-half octaves on a cornet which is the more remarkable because that ability was acquired during the latter part of the last century! Details of brass players of the early 1900s show that several cornet soloists in the USA particularly possessed an extraordinary range. One of these, Ernst A. Couturier, was reputed to have played six octaves (seven Gs); and another, Bohumir Kryl, played (and recorded for posterity) his own variations on the melody *Carnival of Venice* extending over four octaves, with astonishing power on pedal notes.

Other players of that era extending to the 1930s also had a very wide compass including Arthur Pryor and Simone Mantia, respectively trombone soloist and euphonium soloist of the famous Sous's Band. During the 1940s and after, the American trumpeter Harry James and the British cornet/trumpet soloist George Swift (formerly of HM Irish Guards Band) were among eminent brass musicians whose 'stratospheric exploits' excited many, playing their own arrangements and compositions, also established repertoire.

Currently the Canadian trumpeter Maynard Ferguson, Americans Dizzie Gillespie and Clarke Terry, British trumpeters Kenny Baker and Brian Rankine, and the French trumpet soloist Maurice André (whose performances on the piccolo trumpet have popularized that instrument) are notable exponents of high-register repertoire. The sensational American trombonist, Bill Watrous, and some of his contemporaries in USA, also British trombonists Don Lusher and Denis Wick, possess an extraordinary range. And John Fletcher, the eminent tubist of the London Symphony Orchestra, frequently exemplifies remarkably high and low range, also his counterpart in the BBC Symphony Orchestra, James Gourlay.

Range requirements of solo works in the classical forms have grown considerably in recent years, outstanding examples being the Gordon Jacob Trombone Concerto and a tuba concerto (as yet unpublished) by Derek Bourgeois. During 1973 an opus extending over six octaves for tuba was mentioned in an American music journal. . . .

Full ensemble works too have become much more demanding in terms of range which two or three decades ago would have seemed impracticable — if not impossible! Growing use of the fourth valve (tuba and euphonium) and plugs (or valves) of trombones have stimulated this development, also technical advances in manufacture of brass instruments. And the added range has improved overall contrast, appeal and interest of band repertoire particularly.

Range can usefully be developed by all brass players, and the resulting confidence will repay the effort involved. Nevertheless, it is prudent to recognize that high and low note specialization is not of itself a virtue, and only when this aspect is properly integrated into technique can it contribute to musicianship and have artistic value. There is also need to warn against problems with attempts at extreme range production: unless developed *gradually* and with due regard for personal characteristics, tone quality and endurance can be prejudiced and the embouchure damaged.

Exercises for range (and embouchure) development can best be commenced in the middle register, gradually extending into the upper and lower registers. Octaves and arpeggios tongued, then slurred, lip slides and lip trills plus scalic exercises gradually extending upward and downward in varied dynamics are helpful for this purpose. And a moist embouchure is normally preferable to a dry one as, besides air 'seal', it promotes flexibility and endurance. Any kind of strain and tendency to force notes should be avoided, moreover mouthpiece pressure should be kept at the minimum. Air supply is a key factor in developing range, thus air support must be ensured at all times. *Tone quality* is a vital consideration and appropriate care taken to maintain it.

Although change of mouthpiece may sometimes assist in producing a wider range, such change needs to be considered carefully — preferably with guidance from a reputed source. Beware sales-orientated claims such as 'Five-octave Mouthpieces' — even if they are gold plated! Mouthpiece placement change is sometimes helpful in extreme register tone production, but that is personal; experiment, with due regard for intonation and tone quality, will help decisions. Differing mouth formations necessitate different positions for mouthpiece placement. The angle at which the air stream is directed into the mouthpiece affects range and tone, and some players use a 'pivot' method accordingly, i.e. to help production of particularly high and low notes. Use of facial muscles and a liberal air flow with lips vibrating freely, also avoidance of tension, are important facets of this subject.

'Thinking the pitch' of a note before playing it, and positive attack and release are necessary; and once a note is obtained, sufficient air support for its maintenance is vital — controlled, as always, by the diaphragm. *Correct use of the diaphragm* is often overlooked or neglected, yet it is one of the most important aspects of wind instrument performance. Co-ordination of the mind, tongue and fingers (hand, wrist and arm for trombonists) must also be stressed with this need for air support, so that all aspects of performance are unified.

Whether or not a player is able to produce a double high C, if he can play a 'super G' then he has reasonable security for at least a major third above high C: sufficient for most performance requirements. At the other end of the range, low-register notes may be more easily produced if the lower jaw is brought forward a little, and tonguing between (instead of behind) the teeth may help clarity.

Edward Kleinhammer, the distinguished American trombone professor, and author of *The art of trombone playing*, recommends that the vibrating surfaces of the lips should be kept as relaxed as possible; they will then produce more overtones and better timbre, and will vibrate more easily. He also warns against practising beyond the stage of tired lips. Many players find that finger massage of the lips helps to revive them, and face muscle 'gymnastics' may also assist besides generally strengthening the embouchure.

Certain problems are occasionally met which leave players with less than adequate range ability. If difficulties continue after qualified advice and remedial exercises have been tried, change to another instrument may be the only answer. Cornet and horn players so affected have, for example, proved the wisdom in changing to larger instruments successfully — an idea with various permutations.

Just as in the cricket sphere no batsman can guarantee a 'boundary' with every stroke, so no brass instrumentalist can guarantee accuracy and unbroken sound with every note! And some of the most musically satisfying performances have included one or more cracked notes. . . .

Range development exercises must be practised gradually and methodically, and one register ought never to be rehearsed to the detriment of other registers. A true musician seeks to produce a full, agreeable and flexible tone throughout his complete compass, characteristic of the instrument played.

In Praise of the Euphonium

Probably the most versatile of all brass musical instruments, the euphonium is (by definition: The New Grove) a valved brass instrument with a tapered bore of wide scale, normally built in Bb (sometimes C). It is also known as the tenor tuba (notably in the orchestral context) and has a history extending more than 150 years, associated with the ophicleide and the family groups of bugle, saxhorn and tuba. The name euphonium derives from language roots meaning pleasing sound. One of the earliest euphonium references (1830) is in Dr. Adam Carse's book *Musical Wind Instruments* (Da Capo Press, New York) which relates to German-made examples designed by Willhelm Wieprecht, Berlin. Among other continental designers/makers associated with the instrument's early development were Sommer (of Weimar), Johan Moritz (Berlin), Courtois (France), Adolphe Sax and Mahillon in Belgium. British firms such as Hawkes, Higham and Boosey featured later in the 19th Century.

It is significant that the euphonium was introduced into the Band of HM Grenadier Guards in 1851, and the RA Woolwich Band by 1855, also used by light music orchestras in the U.K. later on. Bandsman A. J. Phasey of the Band of HM Coldstream Guards is quoted as having designed a wider bore euphonium than continental instruments used in military bands during the mid-19th Century. Phasey was a very competent ophicleidist, and bass trombonist in August Manns's Orchestra at Crystal Palace; also solo euphoniumist in Charles Godfrey's military band there, he became professor at the Royal Military School of Music.

The euphonium has various shapes: oval, long and short models with upward-pointing bells (left, right or forward direction), with 3 or 4 valves of which the former has a tube approximately 9 feet long and the latter a tube of approximately 12 feet in length. Valves may be rotary or piston type. Some early euphoniums had 5 valves; the purpose of 4th and 5th valves is mainly to extend the compass chromatically down to the first open harmonic, besides giving facility, transposition and tuning benefits. There is also a rare 5-valve euphoium with trombone bell attachment called a doublophone, the name given by Besson & Co. Ltd. Some American companies also made these instruments which were used widely in American military bands; the eminent American soloist Simone Mantia (1873 -1951) played one. In operation similar to the echo-cornet, it enables the effect of trombone and euphonium to be obtained separately. Later development of the euphonium has been mainly by British designers/craftsmen, and British automatic 'compensating' piston euphoniums have a world-wide reputation.

Sharing with the cornet the distinction of being the most important instrument in the brass band, the euphonium is also a principal instrument in the military (concert) band. It has been called the wind instrument equivalent of the 'cello', a fair description in general but denying additional utilitarian values. Often the leader of the lower band (brass and military) it may also play solo or strengthen the melody and other parts, and add warmth and sonority of tone to the overall mixture of sound. It is very effective in florid variations and counter melodies, for example, and its wide application demands varied treatment and imagination. Normally there are two euphoniums in the brass band, thus many composers/arrangers write *divisi* parts, so adding to the harmonic richness of band music. Because of its tonal characteristics it can easily dominate a band, presenting more than a little control responsibility for exponents! It seems that most bands of repute have included outstanding euphoniumists, even if their fellow players could not match that standard individually. Competent euphoniumists can enhance full band sound, intonation, precision and rhythm by intelligent application of the instrument's qualities, and harmonic manoeuvrability adds to its overall usefulness and influence.

Use of the euphonium in all kinds of repertoire, particularly marches such as *Colonel Bogey* (Alford) with attractive counter melodies, has brought it universal recognition. It is also used much in smaller ensembles including the jazz and 'pop' spheres. Confined to but a few works orchestrally, notably Richard Strauss's *Heldenleben* and *Don Quixote*, *The Planets* (Holst), *Sinfonietta* (Janacek) and *Pictures at an Exhibition* (Mussorgsky/Ravel), its value in that area is increasingly recognized. Immortalized in the famous Cornish song *The Floral Dance*, the euphonium enjoys good Public Relations!

Probably the first 'Euphonium Festival' at national level was held in 1970 at Indiana University, USA. American soloists gave recitals and lectures, and massed euphonium events took place. Since then a number of symposiums including the euphonium have been held, notably in USA, Stockholm (Sweden) and Luton (UK), extending its acceptance and popularity.

Artistically played, the euphonium has tremendous appeal, and few instruments can compare with its emotional impact and expressiveness; its mellifluous tone has an intensity and warmth which arrangers and composers use extensively, especially in solo passages and when sympathetic accompaniments are required. The nimbleness of expert euphoniumists, allied to the instrument's distinctive voice which provides a wealth of contrast, has been said to leave listeners breathless! Nor is the euphonium limited dynamically: it can 'sing' sweetly and 'boom' forcefully, soothe and inspire — and even move listeners to tears with its tenderness. The beautiful scoring in *Resurgam* (Eric Ball) and the haunting solo in Gilbert Vinter's *Salute to Youth* are but two of many original band works exemplifying its value and versatility. And it is conceivable that Lalo himself would have welcomed Frank Wright's arrangement of the overture to *Le Roi d'Ys*, if only for the splendid effect of the euphonium solo! The euphonium's compass — well in excess of 4 octaves in the hands of a competent player — is probably greater than that of any other wind instrument, another pointer to its general usefulness and soloistic attractiveness. There is limitless opportunity for the euphoniumist with good technique and imagination anchored to *musicianship*. Awareness (and involvement where possible) of other forms of qualitative music-making will widen music appreciation and performance standards.

Knowledge of the bass clef is most valuable to euphoniumists because it 'opens the door' to more fields of usefulness, e.g. orchestra and military band, besides making available repertoire written for other instruments: bassoon, 'cello and tuba in particular. Use of tutors written for other instruments in bass clef are recommended accordingly (as well as standard euphonium material in bass clef). Relative to comparable solo instruments there is little original solo repertoire available, although a few concerto works (including one splendid opus by Joseph Horovitz) are available with other material plus special arrangements by, for example, Denis Wright and Philip Catelinet published during the past decade or so. The Mozart

Bassoon Concerto (K.191), the Vaughan Williams Tuba Concerto, Suites for Unaccompanied Cello by Bach and numerous sonatas and other standard solo items written for trombone and bassoon are musically and technically satisfying for euphoniumists. An album of Wagnerian Operatic Arias (arranged by Denis Wright) is among repertoire for diploma candidates at London's Trinity College of Music. Development of the 'song-style' and good legato playing, also *intelligent* vibrato use, add to the beauty of slow melody performance in which the euphonium excels.

Several of the most outstanding orchestral tubists and trombonists were originally euphoniumists, thus the euphonium has — in addition to other musical benefits — been a 'spring-board' to the symphony orchestra for more than a few musicians.

After nearly half a century of association with this splendid instrument (those years have included violin and singing studies), playing the euphonium is still my main hobby, with musical satisfaction and joy shared with others!

A Look at the Life and Work of Johann Sebastian Bach
(1685-1750)

The large Bach family of Germany comprised many musicians of whom the best known was undoubtedly Johann Sebastian. He was a church organist for much of his life, and it is not surprising that his music was mainly religion-based; music to him was the apparatus of worship.

In his book *The music makers*, Sidney Harrison says: 'Bach's music often gives us the impression that he actually went to Heaven and returned with the tidings . In comparison, most other religious music composers seem mere incense burners.' The Mass in B minor has frequently been quoted as the highest point of sublimity and the greatest depth of inspiration the world has even known, and only recently it was referred to by a distinguished contemporary musician as 'a tremendous celebration of God in music'.

Not without interest is the fact that the immortal '48' (his preludes and fugues) are commonly called 'the pianist's old testament', the corresponding 'new testament' being Beethoven's 32 piano sonatas. Incidentally, to the delicate series of *arpeggios* comprising the first prelude of the '48', Gounod added a melody, and together they constitute 'Meditation — Ave Maria' (Bach-Gounod).

Bach's music falls into three main categories: organ works; instrumental works, including those for the orchestra of his time; and church music. He wrote extensively, and Wolfgang Schmieder — a German musicologist — prepared a complete index which is now the standard means of numbering, and so identifying, his compositions: the numbers are prefixed by 'S' (for Schmieder) or 'BWV' (Bach Werke-Verzeichnis: Index to Bach's works).

Some of the best examples of the maestro's remarkably inspired compositions are his 'Unaccompanied suites for violoncello' which were published several times during the 19th century, but it was not until after the celebrated cellist Pablo Casals (1876-1973) discovered them that they became generally known. Casals, then only 13 years old, found a copy in a shop in Barcelona — and he called that discovery the greatest revelation of his life.

Line drawing

The suites represent pure line drawing, and there are whole movements without a single chord; but just as the greatest painters were supreme draughtsman, that deliberate limitation was felt by Bach as a liberating influence. Also a competent pianist, it is significant that for more than 80 years Casals began each day in the same manner, by playing Bach on the piano — which, he said, was a kind of benediction on his home. 1950, which marked the bicentenary of Bach's death, saw the first of the famous Prades Festivals, based on his music.

J. S. B. was a fine organist (and violinist) and much of the most outstanding organ repertoire was written by him; recitals of his music often fill churches and concert halls to capacity, and to hear his Great G minor Fugue or similar compositions can be overwhelming! His violin concertos still enjoy performance, if overshadowed by those of other composers.

Unfinished opus

B-A-C-H in German nomenclature are the notes Bb-A-C-B♮, and he used those notes as a theme in the final fugue of 'The art of fugue', an unfinished opus designed to show development possibilities in fugal and canonic writing. It is intriguing to observe that other composers (notably Schumann, Liszt, Busoni and Beethoven) also used that combination, usually in tribute to Bach.

Albert Schweitzer (1875-1965), organist and authority on Bach, said, 'Any room becomes a church when the music of J. S. Bach is being played,' a view point that came to mind a few years ago when listening to Yehudi Menuhin play one of the 'Six partitas for unaccompanied violin' in the Royal Albert Hall, London. The awesome vastness of that place immediately became warm and personal, alive with the combined spirits of a great composer and a superb artist. Such heights of musical experience are rare but they are never forgotten.

Six 'concerti grossi' — the 'Brandenburg' concertos, written for various instrumental combinations — are among the composer's

81

popular small ensemble works and, in common with innumerable other Bach masterpieces, their 'architecture' has fascinated students and experts over the years, besides bringing pleasure to countless listeners.

Increasing popularity of the guitar and lute in recent years has encouraged publication of original music, arrangements and transcriptions, as repertoire for those instruments, not least works by Bach. To 'Mr Everyman' the best known opus is 'Air from the suite in D' for orchestra, usually known as 'Air on the G string', and arranged for various solo instruments and ensembles. The late Dr Denis Wright, made an excellent arrangement of it for brass band which admirably exemplifies transferability of some orchestral music to the brass medium. Eric Ball skilfully arranged some of Bach's music for brass band which is similarly recommended: *Fugue in E♭* (St. Ann); *Jesu, Comfort of My Heart*; and Two Chorales and Final Chorus from *St. Matthew Passion*. There is also a fine album of selected extracts from the 'Unaccompanied suites for violoncello' arranged for trombone by André Lafosse (published by Leduc) which is appropriate for other brass instruments too. John Fletcher, eminent tubist of the London Symphony Orchestra, effectively features the suites in tuba recitals and elsewhere.

Another virtuoso, Maurice André, the French trumpet professor, has arranged and recorded several Bach compositions which he also successfully uses in recitals.

Sir Henry Wood achieved some early recognition for his arrangement of the 'Toccata and fugue in D minor' for orchestra, using the pseudonym Paul Klenovsky, and Leopold Stokowski transcribed several Bach works for orchestra. Such material has few (if any) instrumental barriers, regardless of what the purists say.

Whether preference is for the mighty 'Toccata and fugue in D minor', the splendid 'St Matthew Passion' or the simplicity of 'Jesu, joy of man's desiring' (from Cantata 147), there is always interest and inspiration in the music of Johann Sebastian Bach!

Eric Ball O.B.E., A.R.C.M.

Born in Bristol on 31 October 1903, this composer, arranger, conductor, organist, pianist, adjudicator, writer, lecturer and mystic has become a legend in his own lifetime! His first important appointment was in the Salvation Army Music Editorial Department, and many of his vocal and instrumental compositions and arrangements have been published by the Salvation Army. He also conducted with distinction two of the most eminent musical ensembles of that organization: Salvationist Publishing & Supplies Band and the International Staff Band.

Internationally respected as man and musician, Eric Ball has toured throughout the Commonwealth, the American Continent and Europe adjudicating, conducting and lecturing. And he was for some 15 years editor of *The British Bandsman.* He still contributes articles to various music journals; like his music, his writing is meaningful — and sometimes has a rare sense of humour!

One of the most prolific of contemporary composers, his richly varied output possesses qualities which are universally admired, and numerous works and arrangements by him are standard repertoire throughout the world. By his consistently substantial music written during more than 60 years, mainly for the Brass Band — 'The People's Orchestra' — he has helped achieve general recognition for that medium, and acceptance by the highest music authorities.

His musicianship is also widely acknowledged outside the brass band sphere, and he has directed concerts with the London Symphony Orchestra and the Philharmonia Strings, also featured as conductor with well known choral ensembles.

Of compositions published by the Salvation Army, *The King of Kings, Exodus, Songs of the Morning* and *The Triumph of Peace* number among several classics. Solo material has been relatively less, but *A Song of Faith* (euphonium), *The Challenge* (cornet or trumpet), *Glory to His Name* and *Clear Skies* (cornet) are highly esteemed and played regularly. Compositions published elsewhere include many testpieces, e.g. *High Peak, Journey into Freedom, Kensington Concerto, Main Street, Sinfonietta — The Wayfarer, Sunset Rhapsody, Tournament for Brass* and the incomparable *Resurgam* (also subsequently published by the Salvation Army); although used as testpieces, these works have considerable concert attraction and are frequently programmed. Much descriptive music has flowed from his remarkably fertile mind such as *Devon Fantasy, Indian Summer* and *Petite Suite de Ballet* whose popularity (in common with many of his compositions) has necessitated several editions. Arrangements by Eric Ball include Themes from Symphonies 1 and 9 of Beethoven — and Tchaikovsky's 5th, Rubenstein's *Melody in F, Jesu, Comfort of My Heart* (J. S. Bach) and works by Elgar, Bliss and Sullivan. Some fine original compositions for band and choir, notably *A Christchurch Cantata,* and solos such as *Legend* (trombone and piano, also euphonium and band) and *September Fantasy* (horn and band) are outstanding examples of his inspiration as a composer — also his masterly scoring which is often quoted as a model.

The latter part of World War II was spent touring as a pianist-accompanist with E.N.S.A., then he became professional conductor of Brighouse & Rastrick Band with whom he won the National Championship in 1946. In 1948 and 1952 he won the British 'Open' Championship (Belle Vue) with C. W. S. (Manchester) Band, and that same Championship with Ransome & Marles Band in 1951. Eric Ball's strong influence on the Brass Band is primarily its development as 'an instrument for fine music-making' (his own description), moreover he has written repertoire for bands of all grades: from school and village ensembles to the finest championship class bands!

The Queen's Birthday Honours List of 1969 announced the award of O.B.E. (Civil List) to E. W. J. Ball — Composer, Adjudicator and Conductor. That news brought joy to countless friends, band enthusiasts and musicians generally who have known and appreciated him and his work.

Eric Ball continues his substantial musical (and other) activities, and well-merited tributes were paid to him at the time of his 80th birthday (October, 1983) with special concerts, also an appearance at the National Brass Band Contest Festival.

It would be remiss not to mention his wife Olive who has nobly supported him throughout his long, successful career.

Harry Barlow

On 15 June, 1932, Harry Barlow, 'the Casals of the Tuba', died at the age of 61 years. Tuba Professor at London's Royal Academy of Music and one of the most outstanding wind instrumentalists this country ever produced, he had a distinguished career. In common with many brass players, the brass band was for him a 'spring board' to the orchestral profession. As a teenager he played euphonium in various bands including Rishton (then conducted by the famous Alec Owen), Accrington (under John Gladney) and Besses o' th' Barn. He had a fine reputation at that time as a euphonium soloist, his remarkable range, control and artistry bringing him national recognition. During his early twenties he considered the possibility of turning professional and, after initial orchestral experience with lesser ensembles, he joined the Hallé Orchestra on tuba in 1894 during Sir Charles Hallé's last season; he retired from that orchestra in 1930 and became a founder member of the BBC Symphony Orchestra the same year.

Besides playing in the foremost British orchestras including the London Philharmonic, London Symphony and Royal Opera House, Covent Garden, Mr. Barlow featured on tuba with some of the finest continental ensembles. His wealth of operatic and orchestral experience brought him into close contact with the world's leading conductors and artists, enhancing his stature as a teacher and adjudicator as well as performer on his chosen instrument. He was a member of King George V's Band at the coronation in 1911 when among fellow members were Ernest Hall (trumpet) and Jesse Stamp (trombone). In 1912 he toured the USA with the London Symphony Orchestra and played by invitation at the Beyreuth Festivals on several occasions.

Harry Barlow was probably the first great known exponent of the tuba and he did much to gain recognition and status for the instrument. According to reports published during his lifetime and since, there can have been few brass players who have earned such international eminence. A perfectionist, he used to practise arpeggios, tone control and other exercises before concerts and even during concert intervals! He was very interested in instrument construction and he made various recommendations for design improvements; information indicates that approximately 14 tubas were specially made for him (most — or all — by Besson), the last of which is a 5-valve non-compensated model currently owned by John Fletcher of the London Symphony Orchestra.

Evidently he used an ivory mouthpiece which was the subject of a joke concerning a rival tubist. This rival had been teased for some considerable time by his colleagues in the orchestra concerning Barlow's formidable musicianship and technique, when one of his tormentors mentioned Barlow's ivory mouthpiece. The poor fellow just could not listen to any more about Barlow; 'And I suppose he shot the b----- elephant too!' was his exasperated reply. . . . That ivory mouthpiece is now in the possession of Stuart Roebuck, the Hallé Orchestra's tuba player, who is also the proud owner of two tubas specially constructed for the maestro.

Barlow was also a renowned band conductor, and among ensembles he directed were Besses o' th' Barn, Irwell Springs and Leicester Imperial. In 1927 he took Irwell Springs Band to London to play, with an orchestra of 150, a performance of the Berlioz Requiem in the Royal Albert Hall. He was acclaimed as a band trainer, even if his methods were uncoventional at times. Reports show that very little playing was done at some of his rehearsals, 'the proceedings taking the form of a lecturette' with Barlow telling his bandsmen just what the music suggested and what was required from them! He also wrote articles on conducting and performance technique, and frequently appeared as an adjudicator at Belle Vue and comparable venues where his analytical mind and wide musical knowledge were well applied. Among honours accorded him was being presented to King George V at Knowsley when his Majesty paid tribute to 'the beautiful music' played by Besses o' th' Barn Band. Contemporary journals suggest he was particularly aware of the need for bands to have good public relations and he nurtured this idea, often arranging for his bands to give their services to worthy causes. He was insistent that bands directed by him should have the best music available — and play it in matching style! Barlow's love of operatic music is expressed in at least one published arrangement, a euphonium solo titled 'I Capuletti' (Bellini); he also arranged several unpublished band items.

It was the late Gerard Hoffnung (1925-1959), himself a fine tubist whose ability as a world class cartoonist helped popularize the tuba for the masses, who so aptly called the tuba the bass nightingale! During the last half-century its store and repertoire have increased appreciably, due in no small measure to Barlow and dedicated players like him. Well known works ranging from Tubby the Tuba to the beautiful Concerto for Bass Tuba by Vaughan Williams (1872-1958) have indelibly written the instrument's name on programmes presented in small village halls as well as the world's great concert auditoriums. These developments, also the higher musicianship demands on tubists in brass (and military) bands today, would certainly have been welcomed by Harry Barlow!

In addition to being a pioneer and virtuoso of the tuba, establishing its usefulness both in the orchestra and as a solo instrument, Harry Barlow maintained his love of brass bands. He contributed much to the Movement which gave him his earliest appreciation of music.

Eric Bravington, O.B.E., A.R.C.M., Hon, R.A.M. (1920-1982)

Born in Ealing, London, on 22 December 1920, Eric Bravington was virtually 'cradled in brass' as his father Reg was secretary of the famous Hanwell Band, and his grandfather was a member too. At the age of eight Eric began to play the cornet, receiving lessons first from Arthur East, Hanwell's principal cornet, then from J. C. Dyson, a former conductor of the band. Becoming one of the finest cornetists in the brass band sphere, he also studied trumpet with Ernest Hall at the Royal College of Music.

During World War Two Eric joined the Band of HM Welsh Guards as co-principal cornet with Clifford Haines, and many will recall their splendid solos and duets in radio broadcasts particularly. He had an outstanding career as a soloist, winning numerous prizes and awards, and was runner-up at the first post-war National Cornet Championship of Great Britain. Hanwell Band's Quartet, including Eric, won the National Quartet Championship that year too.

Already a member of the London Philharmonic Orchestra's trumpet section, Eric succeeded Malcolm Arnold as principal trumpet in 1948, an appointment he held with distinction for more than a decade. Due to ill-health he finished playing in 1959 and was immediately made Managing Director of the orchestra; he fulfilled that rôle with distinction too for more than 20 years, and he masterminded several prestigious tours abroad. His musical services were recognized by the award of O.B.E. in 1973.

Eric was Hanwell's Music Director for many years, and during that period the band enjoyed considerable success. His constant quest for musical excellence showed in his work with Hanwell Band and the London Philharmonic Orchestra, and his meticulous preparation was exemplary, as player, conductor and administrator. Also a highly reputed adjudicator, his judgement was invariably constructive and his notes always clear and meaningful. At the 1977

National Championships he received an award to mark 50 years service to the Brass Band Movement.

Eric Bravington was a very kind man, a good husband and father, and he encouraged countless people, musically and otherwise. To meet him for but a brief conversation was a stimulating experience: to know him as a friend was positively enriching! After a long, hard battle against illness Eric passed away on 21 August 1982, sadly missed by all who knew him throughout the world. He is not forgotten, however, because his spirit and work live on.

Fred Mortimer *(1879-1953)*
Band Trainer Extraordinary

Popularly known as 'The Left-handed Maestro' and 'The Wizard of the Baton', Fred Mortimer was a student of William Rimmer. Early experience — he conducted Hebden Bridge Band in his late teens after some years as solo cornetist — and long, distinguished service made him an internationally respected figure in the world of music. After Hebden Bridge he moved to the (then) Luton Red Cross Band of which he was bandmaster until 1924; that band won the Thousand Guineas Crystal Palace Trophy in 1923. During World War One he was bandmaster of the 36th Division Royal Irish Rifles band and, although his first love was the brass band, he always maintained a keen interest in military band affairs.

In 1924 Fred Mortimer was appointed bandmaster of Foden's Band. Before then Foden's always had a professional conductor to direct contests but, as his authority extended beyond bandmaster's duties, he became musical director with complete control. The wisdom of that decision was proved by the remarkable successes achieved by Foden's under his leadership, at contests and elsewhere including tours at home and abroad.

Held in high regard as an adjudicator, Fred Mortimer also composed and arranged band music, but his greatest talent was in training bands; his expertise was applied to many ensembles during his long career. He, more than most of his contemporaries, knew the psychology of training bands, and he obtained maximum results in minimum time. A strong impartial disciplinarian, he was also a man of tremendous kindness and humility which endeared him to bandsmen and held their unwavering confidence. When in my early teens during World War Two I played in the Luton Band at which time Mr. Mortimer was professional conductor. During rehearsal a leak became apparent in my euphonium, a fact of which he also was aware. After that rehearsal he kindly took charge of the instrument which he delivered to a repairer he was meeting the following day! It is significant, and a pointer to his good personal relationships, that for one period of eight years there were no changes in Foden's Band personnel. Sterling qualities as a man shone through all his endeavours as a musician, and personal integrity enhanced his stature in his chosen sphere. A practical technician in all aspects of band training, he subordinated technique to musicianship: 'Look for the music, not just the notes' he often said. In musical terms and technical ability he widened brass band boundaries immeasurably.

Foden's Band of the 'thirties had a musicality and consistency that can rarely have been equalled, and recordings made by that ensemble compare very favourably with those made by the best bands of today, even though recording technique has improved so much since then. After a hat-trick at Belle Vue 1926/7/8, a double hat-trick of Crystal Palace wins confirmed the 'Gold Standard', bringing Foden's world-wide fame. My earliest band memories include recollections of the domestic 'hush' that invariably indicated a Foden's broadcast, and woe betide anybody who broke that hush! Foden's, directed by Fred Mortimer, introduced a new conception of brass band sound and artistry which attracted recognition from the highest music authorities.

Father of Harry Mortimer, C.B.E., Alex and Rex, Fred Mortimer and his family have made an outstanding contribution to the Brass Band Movement. He died in 1953, and a Fred Mortimer Memorial Concert sponsored by the BBC was given in Manchester. It was the first of several 'New Music for Brass' competitions which were widely acclaimed. There is also a Fred Mortimer Trophy, a silver statuette of the maestro, awarded annually at the Royal Military School of Music, Kneller Hall, as a prize for brass band arranging; it is included in the School's official examinations. A very fitting idea, it encourages liaison between brass and military bands.

Gifted, dedicated men such as Fred Mortimer are rare. It is prudent to occassionally reflect on the qualities of these giants of the past as 'guidelines' for the present — and future!

Carole Reinhart - A Lady Musician

Many brass instrument enthusiasts will remember Carole Reinhart, erstwhile bandmaster of Miami Citadel Salvation Army Band, U.S.A., whose cornet/trumpet solos — and personal charm — enhanced several concerts in Britain during the early 1960's when she was in Europe for advanced music studies. Her activities included playing as soloist with the International Staff Band, and her brilliant technique and presentation in demanding works such as Haydn's *Trumpet Concerto* and *Tucker* (Erik Leidzén) were outstanding qualities.

Since then she has progressed considerably in the music profession, and now (following her marriage to Manfred A. Stoppacher, a trumpeter, arranger and composer) works with her husband in Western Germany. It is of interest to mention that Carole was married on Christmas Day 1972 at the First Congregational Church of Palm City, Florida, the ceremony having been conducted by Captain Philip Needham, a former member of her band in Miami. Captain Needham and his wife, Carole and Manfred were co-students at Vienna's Academy of Music.

Carole's education began in Roselle, New Jersey, and her musical talent was recognised very early. Born into a musical family where her mother was a pianist and trombonist, she played cornet duets with her brother Rolfe (now a medical practitioner in California) at the age of five.

In numerous ways her remarkable career compares with that of Maisie Wiggins (née Ringham), the eminent British trombonist, and she featured at the well known Star Lake Music Camps in U.S.A. and also worked with the late Erik Leidzén. When a student at Miami University, Carole was named National College Queen of America, furthermore at graduation she received a Fulbright Scholarship which enabled her to go to Europe. Her qualifications include a B.A. (Miami) and music degrees from New York's Juilliard School of Music and the Music Academy, Vienna. Virtually all her academic honours have been obtained through scholarships, indicating her ability and industry.

An internationally reputed soloist, Carole has played in major concert halls in Canada, U.S.A., South Africa, East and West Europe, Britain and Australia. During studies for her Master's degree in music, she was first trumpet with the Boston Women's Symphony Orchestra, and she appeared as soloist on American national radio and television networks; additionally she has played trumpet with the Radio City Music Hall Symphony Orchestra, New York, and well known European ensembles such as the Hamburg Symphony and Salzburg Mozart Orchestra. A competent lecturer on brass instrument performance, she was principal trumpet in her own brass ensemble with which she toured and lectured extensively. Altogether Carole plays eight instruments including the harp!

Featured soloist on a Deutsche Grammophon ('Début' series) LP record issued in 1973, Carole's fame has continued to grow — including a most memorable guest soloist appearance at the National Brass Band Festival Concert in London's Royal Albert Hall, 1976, plus many engagements as soloist-lecturer since then.

In a hard and very competitive profession which takes toll of mature men, it is significant that Carole has achieved so much. Clearly her artistry and success are influenced by her purposeful outlook on life — and high personal integrity standards.

John Philip Sousa *(1854-1932)*
The World's Best Known Bandmaster

John Philip Sousa, the American 'March King', was one of ten children born of a Portuguese father and a German mother in Washington D.C., USA. The family name really was Sousa and not, as occassionally suggested, 'So' with 'USA' added for patriotic reasons! His father was a trombonist with the U.S. Marine Band, and he joined that ensemble at the age of 13 after running away from home to join a circus. He left the U.S. Marine Band at the age of 16 to work in variety theatres when he was able to play the trombone, violin and piano; the violin was the instrument on which he excelled.

Early in life he discovered his ability to write music such as ballets, operas, songs and works for violin, piano and orchestra, but it was his marches — ultimately numbering 140 — which made him famous. His first success was *The Gladiator* march, one of many examples of martial music thrilling not only his countrymen but people throughout the world. He also wrote several books including an autobiography, *Marching Along*, and three novels.

In 1880 he became leader of the U.S. Marine Band which he made into one of the finest musical ensembles and a major attraction in Washington under his imaginative, compelling leadership. He built up the band's library to contain the best repertoire available, and he enlarged membership — also musicians' pay!

During 1892 he left the U.S. Marines to form his own civilian band in Chicago, attracting some of America's most eminent instrumentalists, e.g. Herbert L. Clarke, Frank Simon and Del Staigers (cornet), Arthur Pryor (trombone), Simone Mantia (euphonium) and William Bell (tuba), as well as players from abroad. Sousa's Band became a tremendous success, numbering up to 100 musicians, touring the USA and other countries, also completing a prestigious world tour, 1910/11. The band played

Sousa's own compositions and arrangements, and other repertoire, with sensational effect, added to which was a hitherto unmatched standard of showmanship — in the best sense of that word. 'Four concerts a day for up to two months at a stretch' was an indication of the band's popularity — and power! Special trains were hired to transport the band throughout the USA, and in the 39 years of its existence it made four European tours and visited most of the world's great cities, in addition to the world tour already mentioned. The band continued until 1930.

Some of Sousa's showmanship ideas included stand-up sectional features, cutting out the brasses in the middle of a work and getting the clarinets to play down an octave; gunshots were also used to impress listeners and to dramatize concerts! Sousa's own unique interpretation of his *El Capitan* march, often used as an encore, was a particular favourite, and the impact of instrumental and dynamics' changes added to the overall effect.

Admired by, and a friend of, numerous orchestral conductors and players, Sousa also had brass band contacts, especially within the Salvation Army for which he wrote *The Salvation Army* march. It contains a song melody written by the Army's founder, William Booth, whom Sousa met on several occasions. That march was written for the Army's golden jubilee celebrations in New York and was played by massed bands comprising 300 musicians, under the maestro's direction, before a crowd of some 10,000 people who gave him a standing ovation; he was then aged 76.

Sousa has been described as ebullient, dynamic and vital; and conductor Leopold Stokowski said he was not an aggressive man, his driving principle being to play what the people wanted. Patriotic and religious, Sousa believed he was 'guided'. He possessed considerable administrative and musical organization ability, plus a remarkable rapport with audiences as well as his musicians who had complete confidence in him. He was about 5 feet 7 inches tall and always dressed immaculately; at one stage in his career he grew a beard and moustache to make him look older, but he later shaved off the beard. A real celebrity who liked the limelight, he tended to be aloof from his musicians who called him Mr. Sousa or 'The Guvnor'; he was never mean but he worked them to the limit. A keen disciplinarian, he always stressed presentation quality and punctuality. He was an important man in the history of his country and was said to have been 'the right man at the right time'. He clearly knew (and exploited fully) the psychology of his chosen form of musical expression which, coupled with a sparkling personality and discerning mind, helped him become the world's best known bandmaster. Sousa's dictum 'A march should make even a man with a wooden leg step out' will, no doubt, live as long as his music!

In 1917 America entered World War I, and Sousa volunteered to train bands. He was commissioned in the U.S. Navy where he trained bands for two years.

Sousa compares with Britain's Kenneth Alford (Major F. J. Ricketts, Royal Marines): he similarly wrote many marches including the splendid *Colonel Bogey* whose theme came to the composer during a game of golf, hence its title. Among Sousa's indestructible marches are *Semper Fidelis, Washington Post* and *The Stars and Stripes Forever*. Such material typified American feelings and outlook, furthermore he had a natural inspiration and facility for writing music at any time: it virtually flowed from his pen. He was master of the march as Johann Strauss II was master of the waltz. It is interesting to note that some of his compositions were published — 'pirated' — in Italy under the name Giovanni Phillipo Sousa, as he personally discovered during a holiday in that country!

Broadcasting and recording were long resisted by Sousa, and he coined the phrase 'canned music' as early as 1910. He did, however, make a few broadcasts and records near the end of his colourful career, and the latter are now collectors' items.

In addition to musical interests, Sousa was a marksman with a large collection of guns. An expert horseman, he was also a zealous baseball fan and he wrote *The National Game* march in its honour. With so many interests to control he was necessarily a highly organized person and an efficient businessman, and according to reports things just seemed to happen without any hitches!

Sousa enjoyed personal acquaintance with numerous of his eminent musical contemporaries among whom were Irving Berlin and Camille Saint-Saëns. He wrote music for famous people, also events such as state and national exhibitions. Countless honours given to him included the MVO, awarded by King Edward VII during one of his tours, and he is commemorated on an American postage stamp.

'The March King' died aged 77 on 5 March 1932, leaving behind numberless tunes and a unique record of bandmastership.

Dr. Denis Wright, *O.B.E., Hon. R.A.M. (1895-1967)*

News of the death of Dr. Denis Wright came as a shock to countless musicians in this country and overseas, perhaps most of all to members of brass and military bands who have played his many fine original works and arrangements which form an integral part of the standard repertoire.

To those who were privileged in knowing him personally, Denis Wright was a man whose competence and integrity were never questioned. Whether successful or not at competitive music events he adjudicated, it was always a pleasure — and educational — to read his beautifully written notes. His conducting was similarly delightful, unostentatious and *meaningful.*

For more that 40 years he championed the Brass Band, raising its musical standing to heights previously unknown, and his craftsmanship as arranger and composer for both Brass and Military Band became almost legendary. He introduced several famous musicians to the Brass Band medium, to compose original works and conduct at band concerts, and he wrote a number of books about the Brass Band, establishing himself as the foremost authority on the subject. Founder of the National Youth Brass Band (a band equivalent of the National Youth Orchestra) he directed most of its training courses when something like 100 selected boys and girls were, within a few days, regularly moulded into an ensemble comparable with the world's finest youth bands, choirs and orchestras.

Denis Wright was a man of considerable character and vision, and he was a great inspiration to all those with whom he came into contact. He was able to simplify the most difficult problems relating to performance, composition, conducting, arranging and teaching, and he was always willing to help anybody, regardless of status. The BBCs first Brass and Military Band Supervisor, his influence in broadcasting, as well as several musical spheres, will long remain.

In paying tribute to Denis Wright one must not forget his widow, Maud Wright, who so ably supported him, particularly in his work with the National Youth Brass Band.

(This profile was published in Musical Opinion *for July, 1967 as 'Tribute from a Bandsman').*

Frank Wright, *M.B.E., F.G.S.M., L.R.S.M., Hon. F.T.C.L. (1901-1970)*

Frank Wright was born in Smeaton (Victoria), Australia into a very musical family. A sister and two brothers were outstanding singers and another sister won national honours as a violinist. He also studied singing besides music on brass, and he won the Australian Cornet Championship; at the age of 19 years he was conductor of the City of Ballarat Band, and not long after began adjudicating bands.

In 1932 he adjudicated the Australian Band Championship at Queensland, and in 1933 the New Zealand Championship at Denedin. In 1934, shortly after arrival in England, he adjudicated the Championship Section of the National Festival at Crystal Palace, London. He toured England during 1934 as conductor of the famous St. Hilda's Band, and the following year was appointed Music Director of the London County Council (now Greater London Council) Parks Department, a position he held with distinction for more than 30 years. It was Frank Wright who inaugurated the splendid lakeside concerts at Kenwood; with approximately 1,500 outdoor events annually, his duties necessitated personal contact with many of the world's finest conductors, soloists and ensembles.

Professor of Brass Band Scoring at Guildhall School of Music and Drama, he was for 25 years honorary editor of *The Conductor*, official journal of the National Association of Brass Band Conductors. He also edited *Brass Today* (Besson 1957), a technical book for brass musicians. A prolific arranger for the brass band, his arrangements of the Haydn Trumpet Concerto and overtures to *Le Roi d'Ys, The Force of Destiny, The Roman Carnival* and *The Mastersingers* in particular are firm favourites and standard repertoire for concert and contest. A composer too, his original works include the ceremonial march *Whitehall* and Diversions on an Original Theme — *Sirius*.

Former Master of the Worshipful Company of Musicians and a member of the corporation of Trinity College of Music, also brass and military band adviser to the 1951 Festival of Britain, South Bank Exhibition, he was guest conductor at many important concerts and national events. One of the most distinguished adjudicators of this century, he served on an international panel of adjudicators at the 1966 World Music Festival. Brass Band Editor for Boosey & Hawkes Ltd., he fulfilled numerous engagements in the brass band context over the years including musical directorship of the annual National Band Festival of the Boys Brigade at London's Royal Albert Hall.

Soloist, Conductor, Administrator and Arranger/Composer, Frank Wright contributed much to the Brass Band Movement.

A Pipe-smoking Band Secretary

Few bands can have had a more efficient and conscientious officer than our former band secretary. He was an excellent administrator and took a keen interest in all band affairs, furthermore he often helped when personal difficulties arose. Although not a playing member, he attended most rehearsals: and that caused a big problem because he was an inveterate pipe-smoker with a taste for the strongest tobacco!

The secretary's smoking habit brought discomfort to our conductor, and sore throats plus breathing troubles to players. Shortly after rehearsals commenced, smoke clouds would gradually reach the trombone section then move inexorably on to surround the rest of the band. The offending practice was discreetly mentioned to the secretary on numerous occasions but to no avail — it was truly a case of 'Take me, take my pipe' . . . One member took legal advice with a view to the rehearsal area being declared a Clean Air Zone but statutory provisions were not applicable to this particular hazard. The offensive 'instrument' was temporarily hidden more than once, and all kinds of unfavourable hints and comments were made about it: smokers' illnesses were luridly described within the secretary's hearing — but our pollution problem continued unabated.

Disraeli said that everything comes if a man will only wait: and sure enough our day came! We entered for a contest at Reading and, because the band coach was full, our conductor kindly transported the secretary, a horn player and me by car. During the journey our subject could not resist 'the weed' and his fellow travellers had the usual smoke hazard with which to contend. . . . On arrival at the contest venue he produced his tobacco pouch, tapped his pipe against a wall to clear it for re-fuelling and — IT BROKE!

We didn't receive a prize that day, nevertheless it was a contest the lads will always remember. . . .

Coda

The desirability of a non-smoking rule in band rehearsal rooms is strongly recommended. In addition to health benefits, it lessens fire risk and enables smokers to economize.

The Harmonious Blacksmith
A Nicknamed Compostion and Musical Hoax

'The Harmonious Blacksmith' is the name given to an air and variations from Handel's Fifth Harpsichord Suite of his first set (1720), which has been used by several arrangers for instrumental (notably piano and euphoium solos) and vocal works. Myra Hess often played her own piano arrangement as an encore. And there is a World War II record of a euphonium soloist with military band (78 rpm), and two LP recordings of the euphonium solo arrangement with brass band. The air has been used in a popular TV advertisement too.

Reference to Grove's *Dictionary of Music and Musicians* and *The Oxford Companion to Music* indicates that Handel did not give 'The Harmonious Blacksmith' title to this opus, nor is there any foundation in the story that Handel heard the air sung by a blacksmith at Edgware!

Early Account

Apparently one of the earliest accounts of the 'blacksmith' story was given in *The Times* newspaper for April 17, 1835, which was reprinted from a journal called *Musical Magazine*. The story was also detailed by a notoriously inventive person, Richard Clark, in his book *Reminiscences of Handel* published in 1836. Richard Clark (1780-1856) sang in the choirs of Westminster Abbey, St. Paul's Cathedral and the Chapel Royal; in addition he was an antiquary of 'Pickwickian acumen'. . . He was the author of an elaborate *Account of the National Anthem* (1822), a comparable hoax and example of faked research about which he was exposed by John (or Josiah) Ashley in two pamphlets published in 1827.

There is a full and interesting account of this remarkable hoax in a book *To a Young Music Lover,* by Charles Seeley (publisher, Arthur H. Stockwell Ltd.) It quotes much of the surrounding intrigue centred on the church of St. Lawrence (Whitchurch), Little Stanmore,

Edgware, Middlesex. Although a tombstone in the churchyard commemorates William Powell, 'The Harmonious Blacksmith and Parish Clerk during the time the immortal Handel was organist at this Church', in fact there was no harmonious blacksmith named William Powell in the area. Furthermore no parish clerk of that name was recorded during the relevant period and Handel was never official organist at the church! Handel did, however, hold the post of director of music in the service of the Duke of Chandos at nearby Cannons.

Additionally Mr. Seeley mentions a Bath music seller named William Lintern (or Lintott) who had once been a blacksmith or blacksmith's apprentice. His habit of singing, whistling or playing the air evidently earned him the nickname 'the harmonious blacksmith' and he conceived the commercially profitable idea of publishing the music under that arresting name.

It is clear that this spurious title and story were originated and 'embroidered' by various people concerned more with fantasy and personal gain than truth. Happily that situation does not affect our enjoyment of the music!

Aloha Oe

The popular tune known as 'Aloha Oe' has various associations, not least to travellers for many of whom it creates mental pictures of garlanded, sarong-clad singers accompanied by Hawaiian guitarists playing exaggerated 'portamento'. To soloists it is known as 'The Priceless Gift', which has been used most effectively over the years, often as a trombone solo; there are also band arrangements.

The origin of this melody is rather intriguing. During 1925 the great Austrian-born violinist, Fritz Kreisler (1875-1962), embarked on a concert tour of Australia and Hawaii. In Honolulu he caused a minor sensation, apparently, among the local people when he asserted that 'Aloha Oe' was not a Hawaiian song but really an old Austrian folk song! Kreisler's disclosure did not go down too well, because the islands of Hawaii have achieved international popularity through that delightful melody, and Hawaiians regard it with understandable pride. Fortunately the shock of the maestro's remark did not last long and was soon forgotten.

When speaking about the Honolulu incident some time later, Kreisler clarified the subject with the story of a violin teacher from San Francisco who had been born in Germany. This gentleman visited Honolulu often and made the acquaintance of the last reigning queen of Hawaii, Liliuokalani, who commissioned him to write a national anthem. He probably appreciated the long distance between Austria and Hawaii, and he took the Viennese song, 'Jetz geh'n wir gleich nach Nussdorf 'raus' ('We'll go to Nussdorf right away' — Nussdorf being a popular suburb of Vienna) and presented it, with a few adaptations, to Her Majesty for Hawaii's national anthem. The violin teacher was subsequently knighted by Queen Liliuokalani for his work in providing Hawaii with its best-known song!

Records show that Queen Liliuokalani eventually claimed to be the composer of the song and she had 'Aloha Oe' copyrighted as her work in 1884.

105

In 1892 the Pacific Music Company of San Francisco published the song with Hawaiian, English and German texts, and the statement 'Composed by Her Royal Highness, Princess Liliuokalani of Honolulu, Oahu, H.I.' was included.

The Carnival of Venice
A popular Venetian tune

A popular Venetian tune, 'O Mamma Mia' was used as the theme of *The Carnival of Venice* variations for violin by Nicolo Paganini (1782-1840), the famous violin and guitar virtuoso.

Since Paginini (there is no truth in the story that he was known as 'Page Nine'!) applied his violinistic fireworks to the melody it has become a subject of variations played on most musical instruments, and the solo arrangement by Jean Baptiste Arban (1825-1889) is probably the most familar to brass players.

William Bell (tuba), Paul Weske (trombone), Herman Bellstedt, J. Bilbaut, Herbert L. Clarke, John C. Hammond, John Hartmann, Harry James, Jules Levy, R. W. Manning, Arthur Remington, William Rimmer, H. Round and Del Staigers number among virtuosi and arrangers who have written variations for solo brass on this theme. Other arrangements are available for solo woodwind, strings, accordion, concertina and even ocarina. There can rarely, if ever, have been a melody that has so admirably lent itself to variation writing!

This tune also occurs as the main theme, followed by variations, of Rhapsody No 9 for piano (called *Carnival of Pesth*) by Franz Liszt (1811-1886). Other 19th-century composers, notably Shulhoff, Bottesini, Herz and Benedict, used it in like fashion for different instruments and ensembles, and there are song settings in several languages.

Massé's opera *La Reine Topaze* (1856) introduced this pleasing melody as a vocal air with variations, and in 1857 Ambroise Thomas based the overture to his opera *Le Carnaval de Venise* on it too.

Several years ago a *Carnival of Venice* solo with variations was recorded with band accompaniment, and the record sleeve specified one arranger but the record itself bore the name of another; the variations actually played were by neither, however! Although the record manufacturers should have checked the details more closely, with so many arrangements available, their problem can be appreciated.

In common with numerous comparable tunes, *Carnival of Venice* has delighted people of all ages with its infectious melodic line, rhythm — and variations. Judging from current indications it will continue to do so for many years to come.

Londonderry Air

('The most beautiful tune in the world')

One of the most appealing melodies ever written — Sir Hubert Parry, a former Director of the Royal College of Music, called it 'the most beautiful tune in the world' — *Londonderry Air* first appeared in a collection of Irish folk tunes published in 1855 by George Petrie (1789-1866). Petrie was an antiquary and amateur violinist who was born in Dublin; he did not record the name of the composer, and regrettably it does not appear to be recorded elsewhere.

Various sets of words have been put to it including *Would I were Erin's apple blossom o'er you* by the poet Alfred Perceval Graves (who also wrote another setting called *Emer's Farewell*), but probably the most popular words sung in this context are those titled *Danny Boy* by F. E. Weatherley. Choirs as well as soloists have effectively presented it in all these forms.

Arranged for virtually every musical instrument, perhaps the best known solo arrangement is that by Fritz Kreisler (1875-1962) for violin with pianoforte accompaniment which he often featured as an encore. Kreisler's recording is still quoted as an example of superb artistry.

The melody appears in the first *Irish Rhapsody* by Charles Villiers Stanford who was himself an Irishman, and in Percy Grainger's attractive orchestral arrangement *Irish Tune from County Derry*. Included in the repertoires of both brass and military band, it has also been arranged for various small ensembles.

One of the most popular items in 'record request' radio programmes, *Londonderry Air* has been successfully used (with and without words) in churches throughout the world.

'Colonel Bogey' — A Splendid March

One of the finest marches ever written, *Colonel Bogey* has lightened the burdens of soldiers (and others) the world over with its catchy themes and delightful counter-melody. And its origin is fascinating too.

Written by the late Major F. J. Ricketts, Royal Marines, who used the pen name Kenneth John Alford, it was probably his most popular composition. At the time, Frederick Ricketts was bandmaster of the Argyll and Sutherland Highlanders, and the main theme came to him when he was playing golf on the Fort George course, Scotland.

Apparently he was unable to attract the attention of some fellow golfers, so he tried whistling to them — using the notes C and A. That note combination fired his imagination, and the march grew from there, the 'Bogey' part of its title deriving from the golf term! Further popularity was achieved by this march being used as the theme tune for the film *Bridge on the River Kwai*.

Britain's answer to America's John Philip Sousa, Major Ricketts became known as 'The British March King', and his marches are among the world's best sellers. He died in 1945 at the age of 65.

More Marches, Please!

For sheer musical inspiration there can be little (if anything) to compare with a competent band playing a good march. Environment and heredity may influence bandsmen's feelings on the subject, but observations suggest that the uplifting effect of rousing martial music is not confined to bandsmen only. Whether personal preference is for the marches of Alford or Sousa, Coles or Rimmer, there seems to be a general response to, and appreciation of, lilting march melodies. And it is not without significance that music requested by radio listeners, played by orchestras as well as bands, usually includes a high percentage of marches.

Martial music originated, no doubt, as an adjunct to warfare: from the primitive warriors of Man's early history to the sophisticated soldiers of modern times, all have been stimulated by this music form. A marching tune — played, sung or even whistled — makes a long, hard journey 'shorter' and more tolerable; it also encourages greater effort. Happily such music is not limited to war and associated matter! Marches brighten outlook, 'put zip into our step' and generally add to life's enjoyment. Without *Colonel Bogey, Semper Fidelis, Under Two Flags* and *The Cossack*, for example, our repertoire would lack much of its appeal and colour.

No less a person than Winston Churchill recognized the therapeutic value of martial music. During the dark days of 1940, when many bandsmen had been killed or were prisoners of war, he ordered the re-formation of military bands. The results of that order raised morale immeasurably. One of my most outstanding musical memories is of H. M. Welsh Guards Band playing marches in the Oxford Street area of London during 1941, just a few hours after a heavy air raid. The benefits of that musical contribution were shown in the unforgettable reactions of listeners, several of whom had worked in rescue and allied activity throughout the previous night's attack. Many will remember the war-time performances of the organist Sandy

MacPherson, who often played marches in radio programmes, notably when normal services had broken down; that too restored self-confidence and hope for countless listeners. Reflection on current events indicates such music has comparable relevance today.

John Philip Sousa, the March King, said 'A march should make even a man with a wooden leg step out,' surely a recommendation in itself! Not long ago a London Tourist Board spokesman voiced the need for 'more massed bands marching through London,' confirming their popularity. Clearly the thrilling sight — and *sound* — of bands marching in Britain's cities and towns are outstanding features that delight visitors as well as residents. Qualitative martial music is an integral part of our cultural heritage and, contrary to viewpoint held in some quarters, it requires *musicianship* if it is to be effective. . . .

Marches comprise a consequential part of band repertoire which we all too frequently neglect, hence the request: more marches, please!

Music — A Creative Activity

The late Sir Malcolm Sargent (1895-1967) wrote, 'It is one of the interesting and thrilling pleasures of the musician to realise that music is not only for the professional and for the concert hall but that it has a willing duty to fulfil to the amateur and the home.' Sir Malcolm further indicated that on occasions the dullest and least demonstrative of us feels an urge to burst into song!

From time immemorial, music has played a part in most facets of man's development, literally from the cradle to the grave. The early scriptural psalmists recognised the value of making 'a joyful noise', and Igor Stravinsky (1882-1971) said the true position of music is at the centre of human culture. In most educational systems, music has a prominent place: from percussion/recorder bands and choirs of Primary School to brass/military bands, choirs and orchestras at Secondary and Higher Education levels, for example. Music also has health benefits, and therapeutic value — one of its most important aspects — has dramatic results in many cases of mental/physical illness and handicap. Of all the arts, we are told that music is the best agent for equal development and co-ordination of the intellect, the intelligence and the emotions. The very 'Rhythm of Life' is enhanced by music of quality, improving character and self-expression.

Radio and television, concert hall and theatre productions, outdoor entertainment, etc., constitute a wide range of professional cultural activity including music. As a result, however, it is easy to sit back and enjoy other people's efforts and lapse into a kind of 'passivism'. We cannot all express ourselves musically, nor participate in dramatics, sport and home-based leisure-time activities such as bridge, chess, painting and the like. Yet folk who have no such creative interest usually miss a lot of life's enjoyment — and quality! Clearly, the capacity to 'participate' is a precious factor of our heritage which ought never to be neglected; creative listening (different from the 'passive' variety) is part of that heritage.

During the past decade there has been a marked decline in amateur cultural activity, some due to the inroads of professionalism and, even more, to economic stringency. Possibilities of sponsorship are lessening, and cuts in public expenditure are regrettably hitting hitherto widely appreciated forms of amateur cultural expression, sport and hobbies — at a time when their influence is urgently needed. . . . There may well be a direct link between that situation and the rise in vandalism and violence. Changes in sense of values, personal discipline and respect, also breakdown of relationships in many areas of our society can (in the view of more than a few experts) be related to contemporary outlook which is often geared to 'get' rather than 'give'. And the world-wide 'Boredom Malaise' has roots in at least some of those matters.

Although not everything in the Victorian and early 20th century era was exemplary, it certainly produced many creative interests. Families frequently comprised vocal groups and instrumental ensembles, and music-making was the focal point of family entertainment in much the same way as television is today. Visitors were unable to leave before they had heard little Jimmy present his latest violin (or cornet) solo, and his sister Mary sing — or play the piano! Poetry and readings also had a place in that 'do-it-yourself' cultural atmosphere, and conversation (consequential and otherwise) was indulged. Mass production, technology and sophistication had not eroded the quality of life to the same degree that we see today; and the alarming incidence of mental illness such as we now have was unknown. Admittedly, the pace of life then was vastly different from that of today, but so also were educational and leisure-time opportunities: these were usually obtained only at considerable cost and sacrifice.

Recently a friend, formerly a band conductor, asked me why amateurs bother to make music when, at relatively little cost, the world's best professional musicians can be heard in person and via radio and television. He had clearly lost the joy of making music, and his rather prejudiced outlook demanded more time to answer than was available. I did, however, invite him to a typical band-and-choir concert, an invitation which hopefully will be accepted.

That several top professional musicians have become closely involved in brass bands, and comparable amateur musical activity, indicates the value they give to such effort — including the joy experienced in participation! Elgar Howarth described the brass band medium as 'the most developed amateur music-making in the world', and its growth over the years shows it is truly music of the people wherein no class or national barriers exist, and all can meet for a common purpose. An artform universally recognised, brass band membership is 'A hobby for life' (Violet Brand: final chapter of *Brass Bands in the 20th Century* — Egon Publishers Ltd.).

Whatever the medium, music is above all to be *enjoyed*. Furthermore, music brings people together!

Musical Hoaxes

Hoaxes of various kinds have been discovered, particularly in the pictorial art sphere, which have embarrassed the experts and confused — and amused — others. The world of music has also had its quota of hoaxes, with comparable results.

Not so long ago it was difficult to achieve recognition in Britain's professional music circles unless one had a foreign name; and numerous arrangers, composers, conductors and soloists therefore adopted names with, for example, 'sky' and 'i' endings. Of interest in this context is the use of the name 'Paul Klenovsky' by the late Sir Henry Wood when, in 1929, he arranged a Bach organ work for orchestra. Shortly after the last war ended, a former military band sergeant began writing and arranging music professionally under his own name but with little success, so he adopted a German pen name, and from that moment his work became popular and is now eagerly sought by publishers in Britain and abroad! During 1948 news leaked out that one of the world's eminent classical violinists had been writing popular songs under a pseudonym, likewise more than a few contemporary arrangers and composers find it prudent to have their work published under assumed names. These circumstances suggest the Shakespeare's 'What's in a name?' dictum does not always apply.

Reflection indicates there could be other reasons for using assumed names. Having regard to the objectionable noises heard in many so-called musical programmes via radio and television today, it may well be a necessity for some instrumentalists and 'vocalists' to hide their true identity, if only for reasons of personal safety. . .

On 5 June 1961 the BBC's Third Programme included a *Mobile for Tape and Percussion* by an allegedly brilliant young Polish composer, Pietr Zak, who was described over the air as 'one of the most controversial figures in contemporary music'. Although taken seriously by the music critics of several national journals, it was admitted ultimately by the BBC that this item was, in fact, a recording made by hitting percussion instruments and producing electronic noises, i.e. not a serious composition at all but merely a random collection of sounds. The idea was inspired by the faintly melodious sounds produced by moving chairs about after a concert, and it developed into a serious hoax *to set people thinking.* After the broadcast, one of the programme's co-producers, a lady concert pianist, said: 'That fake music can be indistinguishable from the genuine is a reflection on certain trends in present-day composition.' She also expressed sorrow for having embarrassed several professional music critics.

Perhaps the most remarkable musical hoax of this century was discovered in December, 1934 when Fritz Kreisler (1875-1962), the great violinist, admitted that a dozen or so works attributed by him to 17th/18th Century composers were really his own compositions. Kreisler said necessity forced this course upon him, and he found it 'inexpedient and tactless' to repeat his name endlessly on programmes. The maestro's admission caused more than a little stir in news media and elsewhere, and it certainly did not please the critics.

During 1967 a report from Los Angeles stated that a famous pop group was to quit recording and would retire somewhere in Europe, and a spokesman for the group said, 'We are beginning to feel phoney artistically.' Whether that decision revealed a hoax is unclear; readers can draw their own conclusions, however.

Undoubtedly some modern composers are embarrased at the thought of pursuing recognisable objectives, and certain avant-garde material described as serious music poses the question: Who is kidding whom? A few years ago an issue of *Encounter* contained an article attacking lunacies which have gone under the name of serious music; concerts were mentioned at which violins were burned, pianos attacked with bicycle chains, and ping-pong balls thrown into wastepaper baskets. In September, 1973, a modern string quartet was presented at the Assembly Hall, Edinburgh; the music critic of a well-known national newspaper reported that players had their bows tied together with a washing line and they jointly used the cello's strings, the leader looking on through a telescope and eventually smashing his own lilliput violin . . .

Total Silence (a form pioneered by John Cage) is one of a long series of variations in the field of what purports to be serious music. Peter Stadlen, the distinguished music critic, in an article titled *Anything*

117

goes now, wrote: 'Even when Antonio Ballista had sat motionless in front of the piano for 37 seconds by way of realising the first movement of John Cage's sonata of silence (which may be of any length whatever), some lemmings clapped.'

A very notable hoax is connected with an air from Handel's Fifth Suite for Harpsichord (1720) known popularly as *The Harmonious Blacksmith*. Reference to Grove's *Dictionary of Music and Musicians* and *The Oxford Companion to Music* indicates that Handel did not give it that title, neither is there any foundation in the story that Handel heard it sung or whistled by a blacksmith at Edgware. The title is spurious, and the story about 'The Harmonious Blacksmith' was originated by people concerned more with fantasy and personal gain than truth. Happily that situation does not affect our enjoyment of the music which has been effectively used in its original setting as well as instrumental (notably brass band, euphonium and piano solos) and vocal arrangements.

The Director of the Consumer Council disclosed in May, 1968 that false names of conductors and orchestras were used by certain record clubs which issued records from taped music. The names 'William Havagesse' and 'Vienna Festival Orchestra' were quoted as having been used on record labels, but investigation proved that no such conductor or orchestra existed! Fortunately legislation now renders people who practise that kind of deception liable to penalties; it also makes musical hoaxes less likely.

Musicians' pseudonyms

It is interesting to observe the use of pseudonyms by musicians, especially during the past century.

First, it might be prudent to dispose of two frequently quoted, but *incorrect*, pseudonyms. There is no truth in the story that conductor Leopold Stokowski was really Leslie Stokes; similarly, violinist Alfredo Campoli was never Alfred Campbell!

More than a few British musicians used pseudonyms during the late-19th and early-20th centuries as a means to achieve recognition. For example, the addition of a 'sky' or a 'stein' at the end of a name, or use of an 'imported name' completely, was often a way to gain notice at a time when many of the best-known musicians were foreign.

And it is significant that no less an authority than Sir Edward Elgar once said of Arthur Catterall: 'If he had not been an Englishman, he would be acclaimed as one of the greatest violinists of our time.'

In his book *The Henry Wood Proms* (BBC publication) David Cox refers to the pseudonym Paul Klenovsky. It was applied to an orchestral transcription the then Henry Wood had made of Bach's *Toccata and Fugue in D minor*, played at a promenade concert on 5 October 1929. Wood wanted to avoid criticism so he used the name of Klenovsky (one of Glazunov's promising pupils who had died young) instead of his own. It was also Wood's idea of a joke against English audiences who 'blindly preferred foreign names!' There was a rumpus in the press when the transcription was submitted for publication and the joke was discovered; however, the success of that transcription was assured.

Bruno Walter, also an outstanding conductor, like Sir Henry Wood, was born Bruno Walter *Schlesinger* in 1876. A reputed pianist, too, he acted as accompanist for Kathleen Ferrier, the contralto singer.

One of the biggest musical hoaxes of this century was disclosed in December 1934, when the eminent violinist Fritz Kreisler admitted that a dozen or so works attributed by him to composers of the 17th and 18th centuries were really his own compositions! He said necessity forced the use of pseudonyms upon him, and he found it inexpedient and tactless to repeat his name endlessly on programmes'. That affair also caused a rumpus, and it particularly annoyed the professional critics.

Yet another eminent violinist, Jascha Heifetz, features in this subject, for in 1948 news leaked out that he had been writing popular songs under the pseudonym Jim Hoyt, notably keeping his own initials. It is intriguing to note that Jascha Heifetz and Fritz Kreisler shared the same birthday, 2 February; furthermore, each of their names in this form contains 13 letters.

Philip Heseltine (1894-1930) used the pen name Peter Warlock for compositions and many articles on music, but his published books (including one on Delius) bore his own name as author.

The American composer Aaron Copland was born with the family name Kaplan; and Paul Creston, also American, was named Joseph Guttoveggio at birth.

The well-known pianist/conductor/music critic Antony Hopkins was born Antony Reynolds. And another outstanding contemporary British musician, Elgar Howarth, uses an anagram of his name — W. Hogarth Lear — for many of his compositions.

Composer/conductor/pianist Edward Gregson, like Howarth, associated with the brass band movement, has written some works under the pseudonym Robert Eaves. Edrich Siebert, also a familiar name to band and orchestral musicians, is the pseudonym used by Stanley Masters; a former military band sergeant, he is one of today's most prolific light music arrangers and composers.

Another musician connected with brass bands and composer of the famous 'echo' cornet solo *Alpine Echoes* was Eli Smith; he adopted the pseudonym Basil Windsor. And the true family name of the brilliant arranger, Gordon Langford, is Colman.

Sir Edward German, the eminent Welsh composer whose most successful work was the operetta *Merrie England*, was born Edward German Jones.

Michael Maybrick wrote popular ballads such as 'The Holy City' and 'Star of Bethlehem' under the pseudonym Stephen Adams. And Mátyás Seiber, notable composer and teacher, used the *nom de plume* G. S. Mathis when writing for the piano accordion. Similarly, Arnold Bax used the name Dermot O'Byrne for his literary works.

The real surname of successful operetta composer Jacques Offenbach is given as Eberst, Wiener or Levy in *The Concise Osford Dictionary of Music*. He apparently took the name Offenbach because his family came from Offenbach-am-Main.

Palestrina's real name was Giovanni Pierluigi, and he also adopted the name Palestrina from his birthplace; and another early composer, G. P. Telemann, used the name Melante (a quasi-anagram of his name) for some compositions.

The Guinness Book of Music Facts and Feats says the composer with most pseudonyms was the late Victorian writer of ballads and salon pieces, Charles Arthur Rawlings, of whom 45 are listed. That same edition reports, however, that the American hymn-composer Philip Paul Bliss is said to have disguised his works under more than 60 pseudonyms!

There was a rule that no serving officer in the British Army could use his own name as a composer, thus (for example) the pseudonyms Kenneth J. Alford, Arnold Steck and Jansen relate to Major F. J. Ricketts, Major Leslie Statham and Lieut.-Colonel F. J. Harris respectively.

Several of the most popular music composers, conductors and arrangers have used pseudonyms. The name Isidor (or Israel) Baline will not have much musical significance, yet it was the true name of Irving Berlin, world-renowned composer of songs, film music and show scores.

Albert Ketèlbey, composer of 'In a monastery garden', 'Bells across the meadows' and 'The sanctuary of the heart', sometimes used the pseudonym Anton Vodorinski. And the real name of Geraldo, one of Britain's best-known dance band leaders, was Gerald Bright.

Relatively few singers seem to have used pseudynoms but one who did was Dame Nellie Melba, the Australian coloratura soprano. Really Mrs Helen Armstrong (*née* Mitchell), she took the name Melba from her birthplace. Another Australian, the bass-baritone Peter Dawson, published songs under the name J. P. McCall.

The original name of tenor Richard Tauber was Ernst Seiffert. And another tenor, Richard Lewis, was born Thomas Thomas.

Older folk may remember the singing duo known as Flotsam and Jetsam who were, in fact, B. C. Hilliam (tenor and pianist) and the celebrated *basso-profundo* Malcolm McEachern.

It is intriguing to observe that Colonel Arthur Goldsmith used several pseudonyms (see *Sing the Happy Song* by Brindley Boon, p. 108); a prolific composer, he did not like to see his name too often!

Clearly Shakespeare's famous question 'What's in a name?' merits more than surface consideration!

One Man's Music is Another Man's Noise!

(Good music is that which penetrates the ear with facility and quits the memory with difficulty . . . Sir Thomas Beecham)

After hearing *some* music, one cannot avoid thinking that silence is a beautiful sound! But subject to certain limitations, we have the right to express ourselves musically in whatever way we are able, thus there is need for tolerance and understanding: especially if music appreciation and assessment are to be meaningful. The quote 'One man's meat is another man's poison' has its musical counterpart, hence the title of this article.

If everybody thought the same, nobody would think. And the rich variety possible in just one subject such as music undoubtedly has benefits (problems can arise too, occasionally), whereas standardisation can stifle progress. Furthermore, experience indicates that, in many cases, differences complement each other.

During the early 1960s controversy — and amusement — arose when the then general manager of the Royal Festival Hall reproduced several concert reviews in the RFH *Monthly Diary*. Evidently they were diametrically opposed reviews of the *same concerts* by professional music critics, the intention being to poke a little fun at their expense, but not all of them accepted that intention kindly!

An internationally reputed music critic's report of a trombone recital given at Wigmore Hall, London, in 1975 included reference to 'experimental non-events', which clearly indicated that the repertoire presented lacked substance, quite apart from the questionable way he said it was played. A more recent trombone performance at a comparable venue attracted another reputed critic's observation that the soloist 'did everything except ride the thing' (the trombone), including 'growling, grunting and squeaking'! Admittedly those performances were of *avant garde* material, pointedly called

'Squeaky Gate' in some quarters. Nevertheless at both events there were listeners who *enjoyed* the music and its renditions, ie, in addition to listeners who *endured*. . .

Not long ago a memorable radio programme included a survey of numerous recordings (no fewer than 20 are available) by different soloists of Tchaikovsky's Violin Concerto, with particular reference to: David Oistrakh's long pauses in the main cadenza; the technical mastery of Heifetz, who played more notes than any other violinist in one four-bar sequence; Elman's warm tone and superb phrasing; Ricci's clarity; and what could perhaps be described as the 'high-heeled' (lady-like) style of a female soloist. Although of the same opus, each recording is different, and that diversity has desirable qualities, musically and otherwise.

It is possible to travel to a given point by different routes which provide varied experiences — they may help or hinder — even though the destination is the same. As in life, so also in music.

Musical Clangers

The musical sphere, like other areas of activity, has its fair share of 'clangers': in concert reports, music magazines and programmes, on music thematic stamps and record sleeves, at music performances and elsewhere the proverbial 'bricks' (even foundation stones!) are dropped — with varying reactions.

For example, singing is sometimes misspelt as 'sinning', and not long ago a religious journal called a distinguished baritone 'an excellent sinner' in its résumé of a church concert. Yet another singer was reported as having a wonderful 'vice' (voice) — not in the same edition, however.

Rearrangements, as well as omission, of letters in words can have unusual — and amusing — results, evidenced by an advertisement in a band magazine quoting *Three 'Scared' Preludes* when such preludes should have been *Sacred*. A Friends Meeting House used occasionally for concerts was regrettably named 'Fiends' Meeting House on a music society publicity poster. Also, because of a missing letter 'p', a local authority announced that it 'resents' a concert by a famous symphony orchestra. One printer's spacing error caused 'The Greenwich Time Signal' to appear as an item in a radio programme given by the Band of HM Scots Guards, and a comparable mistake in the daily orders of another military band resulted in that ensemble arriving one hour late at a concert venue!

Overtures

Overtures are notoriously prone to misspellings, notably *The 'Battered' Bride* and *Poet and 'Pheasant'* which have long since been transferred to musicians' patter in that very form. The hymn tune 'Hull' has been programmed as 'Hell' on more than one occasion and, according to information, the opus *Departed Heroes* has similarly appeared as 'Deported' Heroes.

During 1970 eyebrows (and temperatures) were raised when a reputed national newspaper referred to Haydn's *Creation* as that composer's 'Cremation', and the same year a less erudite county journal twice quoted a *Mass* as a 'Mess'. At least three different music magazines have printed *diminuendo* as 'dim innuendo' but, conversely, 'crashendo' is still awaited. Certainly printing gremlins and the like are no respecters of persons if even *Rule Brittannia* can appear as 'Rude' Brittannia. . . .

In 1956 East Germany produced two stamps to mark the centenary of the death of Schumann, featuring the composer's head against a background of music. Unfortunately, the music printed was by *Schubert*, so the stamps were reissued with a Schumann opus in its place! Another music thematic stamp, issued by the State of Ras-al-Khaima to commemorate Haydn, bears that composer's name misspelt 'Hayden'.

Information on record sleeves is not always accurate, and one in my possession states that Brahms was born in 1833 and 'by 1950 he had already begun to compose'! (Perhaps by then he had already *de-composed?*) Furthermore the same sleeve gives Weber's lifespan as 1786-1926, suggesting he was a musical Methuselah too.

Different arrangements of The National Anthem have caused confusion over the years. A massed bands performance once included a simultaneous attempt in three different editions and as many different keys . . . Fortunately the position was quickly appreciated, and no stoppage resulted.

Apparently more than a few red faces were observed when the President of a foriegn state (whose people deposed their King but a few months before) arrived in Paris. As he stepped from his aeroplane a military band commenced playing his country's *pre-Revolution* National Anthem.

Missing-link passages, *fortissimo* entries in *pianissimo*-marked sections, ragged openings due to misunderstanding conductors' preparatory beats: these incidents and many more can be quoted as music performance clangers! It is good that we are able to regard such matters good-humouredly, but they are also brought into focus to *encourage care!*